Learning Language Arts through Literature

THE ORANGE BOOK

By

Debbie Strayer and Susan Simpson

The *Learning Language Arts through Literature* Series:

Copyright ©1992 by:

Common Sense Press
8786 Highway 21
P.O. Box 1365
Melrose, FL 32666
(904) 475-5757

Printed in the United States of America.

ISBN 1-880892-32-4

INTRODUCTION

As parents we watched and marveled at the way our little ones learned to talk. By listening and responding to English spoken well, they were able to communicate quite clearly. The process was so gradual that they were not even aware it was taking place.

It is the belief of those associated with the *Learning Language Arts Through Literature* series that written language can best be learned in the same manner. By reading fine literature and working with good models of writing, children will receive a quality education in language arts. If you desire to teach using this integrated approach to language, this curriculum is for you.

In her books, Dr. Ruth Beechick has confirmed that this method of teaching is an appropriate and successful way to introduce our young students to the joys of reading, writing and thinking. Our own experiences using these lessons with younger children have encouraged us to share them with you. Their enjoyment and enthusiasm for reading and writing is an unmatched recommendation for this method of teaching.

TABLE OF CONTENTS

How To Use This Book

This book provides you with materials, activities and suggestions that will encourage and benefit you as you create a learning environment for your family. Since all families vary, we suggest that you try our ideas and then freely experiment until you find patterns that work for your family.

Let us first introduce you to *Learning Language Arts Through Literature*, which you hold in your hand. After this introduction you will find the following units:

Everyday Words: Each lesson found in this unit contains a passage of literature and learning activities. These activities are designed to help your student learn language skills in their context while developing writing and thinking skills. An emphasis is on grammar skills appropriate for the upper elementary grades. In each lesson the student will either copy the passage of literature or take it from dictation.

When copying the passage, we suggest allowing your student to use the Student Model. Copying material is a very powerful learning activity. It trains a student to look for details, strive for accuracy, and learn to write. After he has made his first copy, ask him to check it with the model and make any needed corrections.

When dictation is used in the lesson, you will need to clearly read the passage sentence by sentence using your voice and pauses to indicate punctuation marks needed.

Since this method may be new for you, here are a few suggestions:

1.   Before dictation or copying, read the entire passage to your student while he listens only.

2.   Begin the dictation by reading one sentence at a time. If necessary repeat the sentence, reading it one phrase at a time.

3.   Instruct your student to leave a line blank between each line so that corrections can be made more easily.

4.   After dictation or copying, allow your student to use the Student Model to edit his own work. At first have him check his work one line or phrase at a time. After each line or phrase has been corrected, move to the next one until all the work is correct. Asking him to correct all work at once may prove to be frustrating for him.

Newspaper Unit: This unit uses the newspaper as a basis for study in research, paragraph writing, studies in advertisement, vocabulary, and much more.

Poetry Unit: By copying, creating, and illustrating various types of poetry, your student will gain an undertanding and appreciation of this literary art. The unit concludes with a written and oral presentation.

Research Unit: A study of your state provides a basis for study in various types of research, fact gathering, note-taking, writing and more.

Journal Unit: The unit begins with instruction on journal writing. It expands to include sign and map making, photo albums, letters, perspective writing and more.

Book Making Unit: The simple, clear instruction for book binding is enhanced with easy to follow diagrams. This unit can be used with several of the other units or alone. Please refer to it as needed throughout this manual.

These units are written in numbered lessons for easy reference. A lesson can take one-two weeks to complete, depending on you and your student. The units may be completed as listed in this manual, or changed to meet your schooling needs.

Several options are included in the units to provide activities for students who are interested in expanding a topic or for older students who use this book.

Following the lessons, is a section entitled **Student Editing Models.** So your children may easily correct their own writing, we have included each literature passage, labeled by lesson number and typed in large print. These models may also be used when your child is copying or editing a passage.

The **Language Arts Skills Index** follows next in this manual. To ensure that skills commonly held to be appropriate for fourth grade instruction were adequately covered, much research was involved in the writing of this book. This information was primarily gleaned from three sources:

You CAN Teach Your Child Successfully by Ruth Beechick and
Teaching Children: A Curriculum Guide to What Children
Need to Know at Each Level Through Sixth Grade
by Diane Lopez.

If your child has a particularly strong or weak area, you can easily locate lessons that will address specific skills using the skills index. If your child receives standardized testing, skills listed on the test may be found in the skills index.

Next you will find the **Bibliography**. This will give you all the information you need to locate the books quoted in the lessons. The selection includes wonderful books that we hope your family will read and enjoy.

An Integrated Language Approach

Grammar, vocabulary, writing mechanics, reading, spelling, penmanship and thinking skills are all taught using these lessons. This section contains many suggestions for making these subjects beneficial to your student and providing a successful experience for him in language arts. We suggest you reread the following sections periodically throughout your school year.

This integrated language arts program has the benefits of a whole approach, with the advantage of the basal methods as well. By working with whole pieces of literature and focusing on the skills, your student has the best advantage for learning skills in an effective and lasting manner.

GRAMMAR

We believe that grammar should be taught in the midst of writing, not as an isolated subject. You may find it helpful to have a grammar textbook for reference. We suggest *Learning Grammar Through Writing*. This inexpensive paperback is simple to use with clearly presented rules and examples, each one numbered for each reference. The grammar sections in the lessons are correlated with *Learning Grammar Through Writing*. The numbered rules and examples are referenced in the brackets [ ] found in the Dictation Lessons.

As your student works on his lessons you will evaluate his progress by his success in the activities. If you believe he needs more time on specific activities for that week we suggest you locate your own passage of literature and use the same learning activities. If one concept seems to present difficulty you may add that to each lesson for several weeks. For example: each week your student may circle the nouns in red, if recognizing nouns is a problem.

During the writing units in this program, we suggest you focus on the grammatical concepts that are difficult for your student. Remember that the study of grammar is to help the student become a better writer. So good writing = a good grammar study.

VOCABULARY

Your student's vocabulary will be enhanced by reading good literature. Reading the classics aloud together is an excellent vocabulary building activity. When a new word is found, be sure to wait until the end of the passage to discuss the new word. Use the opportunity of a new word to help your student decipher the word using the context. As your student works with good literature on a regular basis, he will develop a larger vocabulary and an ear for proper word and sentence usage.

In this manual new words are introudced and the student is asked to write a definition from a dictionary. The purpose of this is to encourage the student to recognize that words are tools available for his use. As he encounters a word, sees its proper usage, defines it and uses it in the activities, he has acquired that word as a tool. Enabling the student to see the "tools" in his toolbox will build his confidence and ability to use our language effectively. In writing definitions, we are not suggesting that the student copy verbatim, but rather to read the definition, discuss it with the teacher and write a definition that is accurate and meaningful to the student.

PENMANSHIP

We recommend the section entitled "Penmanship", pages 124-132, in Ruth Beechick's book *You CAN Teach Your Child Successfully* as a basis for your instruction. Since skill in handwriting is influenced by maturity in fine motor ability, improvement from whatever point the student begins is the goal. If it is necessary for you to assign grades from handwriting, we suggest you compare the student's present handwriting with whatever his initial handwriting was like. Comparing his handwriting to an artificial standard can be discouraging for all concerned. Concentrating on many skills at once (writing, reading directions and grammar) can provide to be a frustrating experience, so we suggest evaluation of handwriting be done only on final copies of written activities.

When your student is working on a creative writing activity, it is important to let him write rough drafts and brainstorming ideas with no concern for neatness, other than his ability to read what he has written. Many third graders will want to compose orally, and will need the teacher to model writing rough drafts and note-taking. Through the course of the manual the responsibility for this initial part of the creative writing process can be shifted from teacher to student. It is always beneficial to discuss the student's thoughts as he is formulating them, and through this process you will enable him to begin to put his thoughts into order for writing.

READING

We realize that every child will function at different reading levels. For the child who is not reading smoothly, we recommend several steps in teaching him to read the literature passages.

1.   Read the passages to your child. Use the Student Editing Models for this purpose, pointing to each word as you read it.

2.   Read the passage again, asking your child to read the passage with you. At this point you can tell how much of the passage he can read with ease, and any points of difficulty.

3.   Spend time reviewing any difficult words, phonic sounds that need review and sight words or "exceptions" that are difficult for your student.

4.   Reread the passage to and with your child until he can easily read it to you. You may want to tape the passage so your child can listen to the tape while following along with the Student Model.

These steps may be used in one day or in one week. The most important aspect in the reading of the passages for your child is to be successful. PLEASE do not put any pressure on your child to get every word right, as though it was a test he was taking for you. Instead use every mistake or problem in the reading process as an opportunity to teach a skill or to provide the encouragement needed for success.

SPELLING

In her book *You CAN Teach Your Child Successfully*, Ruth Beechick describes three approaches to teaching spelling. She describes the common word approach, which textbooks use to make lists of most commonly used words. The second approach to spelling is the phonics approach, where lists are based on phonetic patterns and spelling rules. The third approach consists of spelling lists made up of words your student misspells in his writing.

Based on the above information, we recommend several methods for teaching spelling.

1. Observe your student during the reading and writing of the activities to identify five or six words that are difficult for him. As you work with the activities you can highlight these words. Identify vowel sounds, word families, endings, blends or any other distinctive aspect of the words as you work with them.

2. After the final dictation or test taken at the end of all activities on a passage or topic, any misspelled words (up to six) may be added to the teacher's master list of spelling words for the student. These words can be used as a spelling list for the following week. Using this method, the date of mastery is written on the master list by the teacher. Again, evaluation of the mastery may be determined by observation, a spelling test or use of the word in dictation or writing. It may take several weeks for a word to be mastered by your student. The master list may be reviewed periodically.

If you feel you need further guidelines for spelling, we recommend Ruth Beechick's book.

THINKING SKILLS

Thinking skills are developed throughout the activities in this manual. Anytime a student is asked to respond to the literature with discussion, writing, drawing or completing an activity, your student is developing his thinking skills. This is particularly evident when writing is involved. Writing sentences describing how he would solve a problem will be a challenge to your student. It is very important for you to discuss your student's thoughts with him, providing the help and structure he needs to be successful in his task. As he becomes comfortable with the demands of creative thinking/writing, encourage him to work on a rough draft, editing and rewriting as he thinks and talks with you about the assignment. All writers must go through this process of ordering and recording their thoughts, so be encouraging and patient as your student learns to think and write well.

MATERIALS TO USE

To use the manual you will need pencils, paper, colored pencils, drawing paper, a notebook, file folders and construction paper. Any other needed materials are listed by lesson. Frequently in the lessons, the student must find a book he is familiar with, so children's books (either your own books or library books) are needed from time to time.

Previous lessons are often used again, so keep all the student's work until all the unit is completed.

Reference books, such as a dictionary or thesaurus will be used as well as encyclopedias. Availability of these materials in either the home or library is adequate.

"What a beautiful place!" said Violet.
"Henry!" cried Jessie. "Let's live here!"
"Live here?" asked Henry.
"Yes! Why not?" said Jessie. "This boxcar
is a fine little house. It is dry and warm in the
rain."

1.   Read this passage with your teacher. How many different people are
talking in it? What are their names? Copy the passage on your
paper.

2.   a.   Using your paper from yesterday, list three-six words that you and
your teacher decide you need to study this week for spelling. Write
each word one time on your paper. Look at each word and decide
what may be the difficulty in spelling it. Find one or two other words
that use the same spelling pattern as your words. For example:

began -- became, begin

b.   Yesterday you found the names of the three people talking in this
passage. Choose three different colors of crayon, marker or colored
pencil. Underline each name with a different color and circle the
words that each person spoke in the same color. Example:

underline Violet in purple
circle the words *What a beautiful place!* in purple.

Continue throughout the passage.

c.   Look at the first sentence you circled in the passage. Show your teacher the punctuation mark used to end this sentence. What does this mark tell us about the way this sentence was said in the story? (10h) Read the sentence with expression.

Look at your passage and point to every punctuation mark that looks like this one. ! This mark is called an exclamation point. What other punctuation marks at the end of sentences do you find in this passage? What do they tell us about the way these lines are spoken? Is the exclamation point before or after the closing quotation mark? Why do you think it is before it? (10v)

d.   With your teacher, read only the spoken words of this passage. One person reads the words of Violet and Henry, the other person reads the words of Jessie. Use the punctuation marks to know how to read each line.

In the passage, three people are discussing something. What is it? How does Violet describe the place surrounding the boxcar? Words that describe a person, place or thing (or noun) are called adjectives (3a). List three-four adjectives to describe your house, pet or favorite place to play. Write one-two descriptive sentences using these words about this place or thing.

Review your spelling words with your teacher.

In the passage, Violet and Jessie like the boxcar and want to live there. Let's pretend that Violet and Jessie do <u>not</u> want to live there. Let's pretend they think the opposite of what is in the passage about the boxcar. Instead of "beautiful", how would Violet describe the place? Use your thesaurus for help in finding opposite meaning words or antonyms for the describing words used in the passage.

Read the passage using the antonyms and make it sound like Violet and Jessie do not want to live in the boxcar.

Take an oral spelling test with your words.

5.　a.　Copy the passage or

　　b.　Take the passage from dictation. Check it using the model.

Teacher Helps:

1.　　　3 - Violet, Henry, Jessie

2.　b.　Jessie - "Henry! Let's live here!
　　　　Jessie - "Yes! Why not?
　　　　This boxcar is a fine little house. It is dry and warm in the rain.
　　　　Henry - "Live here?"

　　c.　The sentence is said with excitement.
　　　　question mark? (asks a question) period. (makes a statement)

　　　　before -- it is part of the sentence

3.　　　a boxcar
　　　　beautiful
　　　　fine, little, dry, warm

4.　　　beautiful -- ugly, awful

That same night Dr. Moore sat reading the paper. All at once he saw the word LOST and began to read.

"LOST. Four children, two boys and two girls. Somewhere around Greenfield or Silver City. Five thousand dollars to anyone who can find them.

James Henry Alden."

TEACHER'S NOTE: A newspaper is needed for this week's lesson.

1.   Read the passage with your teacher. Why do you think the word "LOST" is in all capital letters? Copy the passage on your paper. Check your punctuation and quotation marks with the model.

2.   a.   Use your paper from yesterday, and with your teacher list three-six words that you need to study this week for spelling. Look at each word and decide what may be the difficulty in spelling it. Find 1 or two other words that use the same spelling pattern as your words.

      b.   Last week you found adjectives to describe nouns. In the newspaper section of this passage the children, the boys and girls, are described using adjectives. What are these words? Number words are adjectives because they tell us how many people, places or things are being described. Another noun is described using number words. Can you find it?

c.   Go to a room in your house that has several of the same type of objects. Example: a dining room with several chairs.

Pick an object and tell your teacher two-three adjectives to describe it, one of them being a number word. Example:

Three brown, hard chairs.

Tell her a sentence using these describing words. Example:

We have three; brown, hard chairs in our dining room.

Find two - four objects you can do this with in your house or yard.

3.   a.   Look at your spelling words. Choose a word on your list and tell you teacher what rule you will use to remember how to spell the word.

b.   In the passage, who is reading the paper? Write the word **Doctor** on your paper. Cross out the letters that are left out of the word to make the abbreviation for doctor.

What is added to the end of the abbreviation? Why do you think the period is added to the abbreviation? (10c)

Look at the word Mister. It is abbreviated to be: Mr. Which letters are left out of the word to make the abbreviation?

What type of letter begin these abbreviations? These abbreviations are part of a certain person's name and so are capitalized. Write your father's, grandfather's or uncle's name using an abbreviation.

c.   In the passage, circle all the words that are capitalized. Tell your teacher why each one uses capital letters.

Names of a certain person, place or thing are capitalized and called proper nouns. Tell your teacher a proper noun for each of the common ones listed below:

boy
dog
street
town

4.   a.   Find the table of contents for your newspaper. Locate the classified ads. *Look for the lost and found section.* Read several ads in this section.

           Read several other titles in the classified ads. Find one section that interests you and read several ads included in it. What types of information are included in the ad?

   b.   Pretend you are placing an ad in this newspaper to sell something or to find something that is lost.

           In your newspaper, locate the information on the price of a classified ad. They usually charge by the word or the line.

           Decide how much money you want to pay for your ad and try to write it to cost that amount. Include all the information the reader will need to know if they want your item, but make it meet the limits of your cost.

5.   a.   Copy the passage. Or

   b.   Take the passage from dictation. Check it from the model.

Teacher Helps

1.   Title of newspaper ad -- classified ad

2.   b.   four, two, two
              dollars -- five thousand

3.   b.   Dr. Moore
              octo   a period   to show that it is an abbreviation

              iste
              capital letters

     c.   beginning sentences - That, all, Four, Somewhere, Five
              name of a person - Dr. Moore, James Henry Alden
              title of newspaper section - LOST
              name of city - Greenfield, Silver City

              Possible answers:
                  Tom   Maple Street
                  Spot   Mayberry

4.   Possible answers: description of item, price, age, how to contact
          someone about it.

The children's grandfather wanted them to like his house. He wanted them to live with him all the time. So he had made over some of the rooms just for them.

The children went with him in his car to see the house. When the car stopped in front of it, Henry cried in surprise, "Do you live *here*, in this beautiful house?"

from <u>The Boxcar Children</u>, by Gertrude Chandler Warner. Copyright 1942, 1950, 1969, 1977 by Albert Whitman & Company. All rights reserved. Reprinted with permission of the publisher.

1.   Listen as your teacher reads the passage to you. Take the first paragraph from dictation as your teacher reads it again. Write on every other line of your paper.

Edit the paragraph using the model. Make corrections with a colored pencil. Circle any misspelled words and write them correctly over the circle.

2.   a.   Make a list of three - six of the misspelled words. This is your spelling list for the week. Tell your teacher why you think you misspelled each word.

Example: house -- misspelled as "howse", used the wrong letters for the sound of "ou."

Now tell your teacher one or two words that use the same spelling pattern as your word.

Example: mouse

b. The passage uses the expression "made over" to tell us what the children's grandfather had done to some rooms in his house. What do you think this expression means in the sentence?

Read the first paragraph to your teacher. Think about the children's grandfather. Describe the kind of person you think he is to your teacher.

c. In the second paragraph, the children arrive at their grandfather's house. What do you think it looked like to the children? Why do you think that?

Henry is surprised when they stop in front of this house. He is so surprised that he cries out, "Do you live *here*, in this beautiful house?" Why do you think the word "here" is written in italics?

Read the words of Henry using expression in your voice.

3   a. In the first sentence, circle the word that tells us whose grandfather wants them to like his house. The word children has to be changed when we make it <u>own</u> something, or write it in a possessive form. What is added to the word?

Find three objects in your house that belong to different people and put them on your table. (Be sure to ask permission to use something that belongs to a family member.) Tell your teacher who owns each thing using the following pattern:

This <u>book</u> belongs to <u>Tom</u>.

Write about each object using a possessive noun to show who owns or possesses it.

Example: Tom's book

16

b. In the passage, circle the word "he" every time it is used. Who is "he" in each case? Circle the word "him" every time it is used in the passage. Who is the person that "him" is talking about in each case? "He" and "him" are words that replace the word grandfather in these sentences. They are pronouns, that take the place of a noun. (1i)

In the first sentence, whose house is described? The word "his" is the ownership or possessive form of he and him. Whose car did the children ride in to grandfather's house?

Using the same objects from your possessive noun lesson, tell your teacher about each object using a pronoun.

Example: This <u>book</u> belongs to <u>him</u>.

Write about each object using a possessive pronoun. (1m)

Example: his book.

4. a. In the story of the boxcar children, their grandfather remodels a room just for each of them. Violet's room is white with violet wallpaper, a purple bedspread and flowers on the side table.

If you could have a room remodeled just for you, how would you like for it to look?

Talk to your teacher about the walls, bed, closet, shelves, etc. In your discussion include colors, designs, and sizes.

Write three or four sentences describing your made over room.

b. Take an oral spelling test on your words.

5. Take the passage from dictation. Correct with the model.

Teacher Helps

2. b. remodeled, remade the rooms to look different.
    Possible answers: loving, kind, thoughtful, generous

  c. beautiful, big, much better than expected.
    Henry is surprised by the house.

    to show emphasis

3. a. children's
    's

  b. grandfather
    grandfather

    his house, grandfather's house
    his car, grandfather's car

TEACHER'S NOTE: For this unit on newspapers, you may want to arrange a visit to a newspaper office if one is available. It would be very interesting to see the production process first-hand.

(This activity may be done in two days.)

1.   Newspapers are very familiar to us. We can see them being sold on many street corners; however, we often do not know much about how newspapers began in our country. Look up the names up in an encyclopedia, at the library or in any available reference book. With any needed help from your teacher, read about the lives of these people. Decide what part you think they played in the development of the newspaper in America.

John Peter Zenger
Benjamin Franklin

TEACHER'S NOTE: As the student looks at the encyclopedia or reference material, ask him to tell you how to find the information you want. For example, to look up information on Benjamin Franklin we must first find the "F" volume or listings and then locate his name alphabetically.

2.   Once the information on the two individuals has been found, discuss what you have learned about each person and his involvement with the newspaper. After discussion with your teacher, write at least four sentences about each individual, giving the facts that seemed most important to you. *Zenger - Jan. 22   — Franklin - Jan. 23*

3.   The historical figures looked at in Activity #1 worked for the freedom of the press, or the right to tell the truth in the newspaper. Again, using an encyclopedia or reference books, look up the portion of our United States Constitution known as the Bill of Rights. Ask your teacher for help in locating the First Amendment and copy the part of the amendment that you think would affect newspapers. These amendments were ratified, or made law in 1791, over 200 years ago.

4.   Look through information gathered to answer Activities 1-3, and make a list of at least five words that were new to you. Once this list has been made, use the dictionary to find these words and write a definition of each. Find the abbreviations (letters with a period after them) listed after the word telling the part of speech. Example: n. means noun. List the part of speech for each word defined.

5.   Using the information gained in Activity #3, talk about the effect the First Amendment has on those who publish newspapers. Also discuss what guidelines you think a newspaper should go by if they are free to publish anything.

Make a list of three - five guideline ideas from your discussion. Number your paper and write your idea in a few words; not a complete sentence.

Example: 1.   the protection of the public

TEACHER'S NOTE: For this week and next week's lesson, please make several copies of newspapers available to your child.

1. a. You will be learning about newspapers for the next few weeks. To begin, we will learn the jobs needed to make a newspaper. Look up these three words in the dictionary and discuss their meaning with your teacher:

          reporter   editor   publisher

    b. Look up each of these people in a reference book, book about newspapers, or encyclopedia and read them with your teacher. Your teacher will give you any help needed.

              Ernie Pyle
              Edward Bok
              Frederick Douglass
              William Randolph Hearst

    c. Tell what job (reporter, editor or publisher) each of these people had. Do you think they were good at their jobs? Do you know anyone else who does one of these jobs?

2. a. Look at the copy of our make-believe newspaper on the next page. It has many features of a real newspaper. Find the name of the paper in large letters at the top of the page. This is called the "flag." The "flag" for our paper is *Happy Town Herald.* Look at a real newspaper and find the "flag."

    b. Common names of newspapers often include words like herald, gazette, and tribune. Look these three words up in your dictionary and tell your teacher, in your own words, why you think these words are included in newspaper names. Are there any words like these in the title of the newspaper you are looking at? If so, look up that word and describe to your teacher why you think it was used.

c.   Look on the first page of the *Happy Town Herald* and find the list of where to find things in the newspaper. This is called the "index". Look at your newspaper and find the index. Is every part of the newspaper listed in the index? Can you find the comics using the index? Use the index to find the weather report.

3.   a.   Now that we have begun to look at the newspaper, let's think about why newspapers are published. The index told us some of the things included in a newspaper. Look through the newspaper and, together with your teacher, make a list of the things you see included in the newspaper (i.e. things for sale, sports scores, news about the community, what's on at the movies, etc.).

      b.   Using your list, discuss with your teacher, why newspapers are published.

TEACHER'S NOTE: The generally accepted purposes of a newspaper are to present information, such as current events, to provide a service to individuals, such as weather reports, to provide entertainment, such as comics, and to help people understand information, such as editorials.

4.   a.   What kind of articles do you think would be on the front page of the newspaper? (Whatever the editor thinks is the most important news.) One of the things that tells you which story is the most important story are the very large words above it called the banner. A banner is the group of words that go across the page telling about the story. Find the banner on the *Happy Town Herald*.

      b.   The front page has the lead story. It is the story that the editor thinks is the most important news of the day. The banner is over the lead story. Find the lead story on the front of the *Happy Town Herald*.

      c.   Find the banner and lead story of the front of a real newspaper. Discuss your choice with your teacher. Do you think it is the most important news of the day? Look at one other newspaper and see if they have the same lead story.

Happy Town Herald

FINAL

10 PAGES
10¢

Happy Town, Schoolland

Thursday, May 7, 1992

What's New?

Sports:
Happy Town Bowlers
Take Ten! p. 4

Weather:
Sunny Skies Today p. 10

Health:
Happy Town Residents
Walk p. 2

Index

Editorial

by Ann Sunshine

Town Divided On Trees

The debate continues all around Happy Town over what type of trees to plant on our new street, Sunny Lane. While there is still time, I would like to make a case for planting walnut trees.

Walnut trees are neat and clean, have strong, sturdy trunks and limbs, and produce very tasty nuts. Even though most of our trees in town do produce fruit, and this fruit is also tasty, I think it is time for a change. We must not be afraid to try something new.

Survey: Make your opinion known! Drop by the Happy Town Herald office and vote for pear or walnut trees for Sunny Lane. Results of our poll will be presented at the next town meeting.

Bank Ground-Breaking Ceremony Today

Happy Town- The community of Happy Town welcomes Safe and Sound Bank, with a ground breaking ceremony at 2 p.m. today. The mayor and town council will be on hand to greet bank president, Sam T. Safe as construction on our newest business begins. All residents are welcome to come and witness the dedication of the cornerstone to our town founder, Albie Happy.

This is the model replica of the bank as it will appear at its completion in 1993.

Located on the corner of Grape and Apple Roads, President Safe estimates the bank will employ about 20 Happy Town residents as well as serve all of Happy Town with friendly, reliable banking. The construction company of We Build Smiles, Inc. is in charge of the building, and officials at the company expect to complete construction toward the middle of 1993. We Build Smiles, Inc. is also looking for workers to assist in the project. Overall, Safe & Sound Bank is sure to benefit Happy Town in many ways.

Happy Town Still Growing

The figures are in for the first four months of the year, and Happy Town's population is still on the rise.

As the Line Graph shows, growth was the greatest in April.

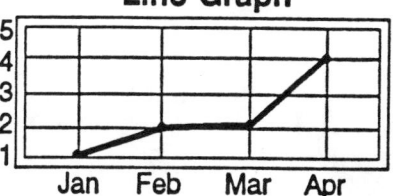

Line Graph

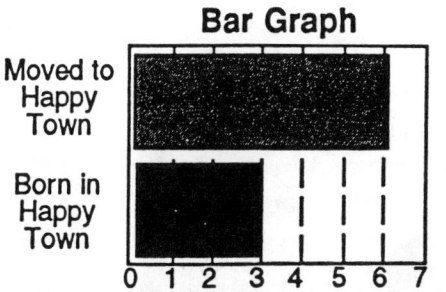

Bar Graph

The Bar Graph shows that one third of the new residents were born here in Happy Town this year.
A total of nine new residents are now living in Happy Town.

LOCAL NEWS

Many Walk For Fun, Exercise

Downtown- On almost any evening in Happy Town, you can see couples, families, and friends out for an evening walk. With mild weather and longer daylight, the streets seem to be teeming with walkers.

"It is a lovely time of year to be outside," said Mrs. Smiley, when asked why she was walking. Mr. Smiley added, "Great exercise, too!" This new trend seems not to be limited by age. The Friendly Family children passed by on bicycles, with mom and dad setting the pace on foot. "We have fun going with mom and dad," said Sally Friendly, age 8.

Dr. Bob Healthy, of Happy Town Memorial, thought it was a wonderful sight to see. He commented that walking is an excellent choice for health and enjoyment.

Walkathon To Benefit Happy Town Zoo

Happy Town Zoo- Zoo owners hope that a new home can be provided for Sally the Chimp, who arrived at Happy Town Zoo yesterday.

More room is needed for Sally, so local zoo supporters are participating in a walkathon Saturday to raise money for a chimp home to be built in the zoo. Walkers are gathering pledges of 10¢ per lap, (laps will be walked around the zoo), with the walkers beginning at 9 a.m. Bring your sneakers to walk, or money to sponsor someone to the zoo on Saturday and help us build a home for Sally!

LETTERS TO THE EDITOR

If you have any questions or comments that you would like to address to the editor feel free to come by the office or write to:

Letters To The Editor
Happy Town Herald
123 Sunshine Place
Happy Town, Schoolland
98765-4321

Dear Editor:

I am the owner of "Henry's Apple Orchard" and I would like to see more apple recipes in the Recipe Section of your paper. While various other fruits are good for baking and other treats, I feel that apples are being left out. I am sure people who buy my apples would love to try some new dishes also!

Bushels of thanks,

Henry

Editor's Note:
Sorry Henry - It was purely an oversight on our part that apple recipes were not often included in the Recipe Section. Please accept our apology, and look forward to many tasty apple recipes very soon!

Dear Editor:

We would like to say that the improvements made to Happy Town's Park and Camping Grounds are wonderful. Our family had been looking for a campsite nearby where we could spend our weekends. At the suggestion of a friend, we camped there last weekend and, after seeing the facilities and recreational areas, we all agreed that our tax dollars had been well spent. Our two children particularly enjoyed the new swimming area and my husband and I were thrilled by the beauty and splendor of the new nature trail. Thanks to our Town Council for money well spent, and a job well done!

Sincerely,

The Camper Family

d. Do you think the size of the letters in the banner means anything? Do you think the editor would use bigger letters for news he thought was really important? Can you think of an event that would have had very large banner letters? Ask your teacher if she can think of any events that had very large banner letters.

5. a. When you talked with your teacher about why newspapers are published, one of the reasons you probably came up with was to tell people the news, or to give them information about what is happening. The first paragraph of a story usually has very important information in it. The answers to these questions are usually in the first paragraph:

Who? What? When? Where?

Look at the lead story in the *Happy Town Herald*. Answer those questions about the lead story using the first paragraph.

b. The other paragraphs in the story usually tell why something has happened and how it happened. These paragraphs usually have details about the event. Read the other paragraphs in the lead story and answer these questions:

Why? How?

c. Find the lead stories in the two newspapers you looked at yesterday. Using the lead or first paragraph of each, tell your teacher the answer to these questions:

Who? What? When? Where?

d. Using the later paragraphs of each story, answer these questions for your teacher:

Why? How?

6. a. Together with your teacher, choose an event that happened recently. It can be something that happened at home, it does not have to be a "news" story. Discuss what happened and decide how you would answer these questions: Who? What? When? Where?

Write your answers in paragraph form, remembering to indent the first line. (6b) Read this with your teacher and make any needed changes.

b.   Discuss the answers to the questions why and how regarding the event. Think of three or four sentences that answer these questions and write them down. Indent this paragraph as well.

c.   A headline is the group of words in larger letters over a story in a newspaper. Look up the word "headline" in the dictionary and discuss its meaning with your teacher. On a lead story, the banner is the headline. On all other stories, the headline is right above the story. Look at the banner and a headline. What is the difference? Find a story and its headline in the *Happy Town Herald*.

d.   Find several stories and their headlines in the real newspapers. Headlines are not really titles, they tell what the story is about. They also try to catch your attention, so that you will read the whole story. Discuss possible headlines for your story with your teacher. Write it above your story in letters that are larger than those used in the story.

Teacher Helps:

1.   c.   Ernie Pyle - reporter
         Edward Bok - editor
         Frederick Douglass - publisher
         William Randolph Hearst - publisher

1. a.   When people read a newspaper, they may be reading it for several different reasons. They may want to know what is happening in their neighborhood, city, state, country or anywhere else in the world. When people are reading a newspaper for this reason, they want to find out the "facts" about what has happened. Look up the word "fact" in the dictionary. Discuss what it says with your teacher and write a definition in your own words.

    b.   Find an example of a story in the *Happy Town Herald* that is made up mostly of facts. Look in a real newspaper and find a story that has mainly facts in it. These stories are usually found in the first section of the newspaper. Think back to what you discussed about what a reporter does. Discuss with your teacher whether or not a reporter should be writing the facts about what he sees.

    c.   An important difference to notice in things we read or hear is to decide whether they are facts or opinions. Look up the word "opinion" in the dictionary. Discuss the definition with your teacher and write what "opinion" means in your own words.

    d.   Find an example of a story in the *Happy Town Herald* that is made up mostly of opinions. Look in a real newspaper and find a story that has mostly opinions in it. These stories are usually found in later sections of the paper. What job at a newspaper do you think would include writing opinions about things that happen? (Editor)

    e.   Now that you have learned what a fact is and what an opinion is, how are they different? Think of two events that have happened around your house. Together with your teacher, come up with a fact and an opinion about each event.

2. a.   One of the jobs at a newspaper is the job of editor. Think about what an editor does and discuss this with your teacher.

b. One part of a newspaper is called the editorials. These are opinions, or thoughts, written by the editor. Find the editorial, or thoughts of the editor in the *Happy Town Herald*. What subject is the editor talking about, and what does he think about it?

c. Find the section of a real newspaper that has the editorials in it. Choose an editorial and read it with your teacher. What subject is the editor writing about? What does he/she think about the subject?

d. Discuss the subject of editorials with your teacher. Do you think people should believe only what the editor says? Do you think people always agree with the editor? Do you think it is all right to disagree with the editor?

3. a. Near the editorials in the newspaper is a section where there are letters printed that have been sent to the editor. These letters tell what people think about different issues. Find the section in the *Happy Town Herald* that has letters to the editor. Read them with any needed help from your teacher.

b. Find the section in the newspaper that has letters to the editor. Read and discuss them with your teacher. Do you see any that you agree with? Do you see any that you disagree with?

c. Since the editor shared his opinion in the editorials, how do people let the editor know what they think of his opinion?

d. Ask your teacher to help you look in the editorial section and find the policy of the paper for letters to the editors. What do they want you to do if you want to write a letter? Are these good guidelines?

e. Talking with your teacher, think of a subject that you have strong feelings about such as homeschooling, your church, or your favorite sport. Make up a pretend letter to the editor of the *Happy Town Herald* and tell the editor why you feel so strongly. Look at the other letters and make sure yours follows the same form.

4. a. If you watch TV, look in a newspaper or even drive around town, you will see advertising. Look up the word "advertise" in the dictionary and discuss its meaning. Write a definition in you own words.

    b. Talking with you teacher, come up with a list of different kinds of advertisements. Look through newspapers, magazines or on television to add to your list. Are just items advertised?

    c. After looking at many types of advertisements, what do you think is the purpose, or goal of the advertisers? Discuss this with your teacher.

    d. What kind of statements do you think are used in advertisements -- facts or opinions or both? Look at two advertisements from your newspaper. Make a list of facts and a list of the opinions you see in each ad.

5. a. Together with your teacher, discuss what you think would happen if something that looks like a fact in an advertisement was not true? When we look at an advertisement, or ad, should we believe everything we see? How can we make sure that what the advertiser is saying is true? Come up with several ways you might check to see if an advertisement is telling the whole story.

    b. Look at the pretend ads on the next page. What do you think is fact and what is opinion? Do you think you are given enough information to make a good decision?

    c. Look through the newspaper and see if you can find any ads that may not give enough information about the item advertised to make a good decision.

    d. Talk with your teacher about something you like or like to do. Make up an advertisement for that thing, place or activity. Make it neat and attractive, including all the information you think would be important. You may use markers, crayons, cut-out pictures or anything that you think will make your ad better. Show it to several people and see if they like and understand what you are advertising. Did they have any unanswered questions?

 **b.** Look at these pretend ads. What do you think is fact and what is opinion? Do you think you are given enough information to make a good decision?

FRAN'S FANCY FANS

- *Perfect for decorating!*
- *Made in 50 colors!*
- *Strong - Lasts a lifetime!*
- *What everyone needs for their home!*

Only $9.95 and up

Call Today!
351-5891

Or Come By!
100 Fancy Street, Fancytown

Come To...
Beautiful Lake Happy!

 *Where everyone is happy!*

$5.00 per person
• Today Only

✓ **Swimming Fun**
✓ **Play in the Sand**
✓ **Get a Great Tan**
✓ **Perfect for the Whole Family!**

* Prices may change without warning.

Teacher Helps:

2.   b.   Which trees to plant
                 walnut trees

1. a. Another purpose for reading the newspaper is to enjoy stories and to read articles about things that interest you. These are called feature articles and are usually not written like stories on the front page about news. Look at the article in the *Happy Town Herald* about walking. How is it different from the story about the new bank?

    b. Look in your real newspapers and find at least two stories that are about things people might be interested in, such as books or nature. Do you think all the people writing these stories are reporters? Look at the end of the article and see if anything is told about the person who wrote it.

    c. Choose something that interests you. Talk with your teacher about what you would want to tell another person about your interest. Write at least two paragraphs that would help others understand this interest. Maybe people will want to learn more or try your activity after hearing about it, so you can tell them how you feel about it.

2-5   We have looked at many different aspects of a newspaper and you have practiced writing many different types of information. For the rest of this week, work on creating your own newsletter or short newspaper. You could make one on your family (what's going on with each member, pictures, upcoming events, articles about interests, news articles, editorials, etc.) or on an area of interest or an activity you like (Little League, stamp collecting, dogs, etc.). Another option might be to make a newspaper about your homeschool support group or your own homeschool.Go through the lessons in the order that we presented them and come up with things like a flag, an index, news/articles, headlines, editorials and feature articles. Look at newspapers and the *Happy Town Herald* to decide how you want your newspaper to look. You may want to do what is called "cut and paste" to give it the look of having information in boxes. Write the information down, cut it out and then paste it where you want it on your newspaper. You can draw boxes or lines around the different sections.

Enjoy the process and come up with a newspaper or newsletter that you can share with others. This may be the beginning of a new tradition for you, your family or friends, this once or at special times of the year like holidays or birthdays.

1.   a.   Using a map of your state, find the capital (usually marked with a star.) Later in this manual we will be writing a report about your state, so you may want to ask for some information now.

Discuss with your teacher how to word a request to the Chamber of Commerce of your state capital for information. Here is a sample request:

Your Address
Today's Date

Chamber of Commerce
Your state capital

Dear Sirs:

I am writing a report on our state and would like to request information on our state. Any information on our state's past or present would be helpful. Thank you for your reply.

Sincerely,

Your Name

Make a rough draft with your teacher. Recopy your letter, address an envelope and mail your request.

    b.   Begin gathering information on your state from other sources in your library. Our goal is to learn about your state and then share what you have learned with others. Collect items that can help tell about your state like a map of your state, pictures, drawings, newspaper or magazine articles. Gather this information and put it in a folder.

c.	As you gather information, reading with your teacher, keep a list of words that are new to you. As you write a word on your list, be sure to look it up in the dictionary. After reading the definition, write a short explanation of what the word means.

2.	a.	We are going to prepare to do some research. In several weeks we will be looking at many different resources for information about your state. How do you gather information and remember it? One way is called notetaking. You may not realize it but you already take notes. When someone calls to speak to your father and he is not home, you make notes to tell him about the conversation. You certainly don't write down every word that is spoken; you only write down the most important facts for your dad. Here is an example of a message you might write:

Dad - Mr. Jones called at 2:00. Please call him back. 967-8199.

This may not seem like much, but if any of this information is wrong or left out, your dad may not be able to return the call.

b.	After discussing with your teacher, make a list of the things that are important to write down from a phone conversation for another person who is not there.

3.	a.	Another way we can gather information is by taking notes on what we have read. Again our goal is not to copy down every word, but to read something and write down the facts that seem most important to us.

Here is an example of taking notes on the facts we read:

It was a beautiful day.
The sun was shining and the birds were singing.
As the girl walked along the dirt road, the sand felt warm on her bare feet.
Summer flowers by the road seemed to call her to pick them.

My notes would be: 1) a barefoot girl
                                    2) walking down a dirt road
                                    3) nice summer day

b.   Reread each excerpt of <u>The Boxcar Children</u> used in Lessons 1-3. After reading each excerpt discuss with your teacher what seems to be the most important facts from each segment, and write a sentence or two telling the main facts from the excerpt.

4.   Together with you teacher, choose a TV show or video to watch or recall something you both have seen. With your teacher's help, come up with three or four sentences that tell the main points about the show you watched. Once you have discussed them, write them down. Reread your sentences to make sure you both agree that all the main points of the show were covered. A brief show (approximately 30 minutes) may be best for this activity.

5.   We have looked at three kinds of information we can take notes on what we hear, what we read and what we see. Choose one of these ways and practice taking notes. Write three or four sentences and discuss them with your teacher.

The Wright boys were friendly. It didn't take them long to get acquainted with the boys on Adams Street in Cedar Rapids, Iowa.

They were getting acquainted with the city too. Today they had gone to see the rapids in the Cedar River. They were standing on the bank now looking down at the whirling water.

Reprint with permission of Macmillian Publishing Company from Wilbur & Orville Wright by Augusta Stevenson. Copyright 1951, 1959 by Bobs-Merrill Co., Inc.

1. Read the passage with your teacher. Write the first paragraph from dictation using every other line on your paper. Edit your writing using the model. Correct any mistakes, circle misspelled words and write the correct spelling above the circle. Copy the second paragraph.

2. a. Looking at your circled words from yesterday, make a list of four -six for your spelling list. Discuss with your teacher why each word was misspelled. Think of one to two other words that follow the same spelling pattern as the ones on your list.

    b. In the passage, circle all the capital letters that are not at the beginning of a sentence and tell your teacher why each one is capitalized. In the first paragraph, put a box around the city and state name. What punctuation mark separates the city from the state?

    Write your address, including your street name and number, city and state using the correct capitalization and punctuation.

    TEACHER'S NOTE: Complete the activity sheet for this lesson, found on the next page, before you begin these activities.

Lesson 9 - Student Activity Page

Color parrot and cut out:

Cut on dotted lines. Fold on solid lines. Apply glue where indicated and attach to make a box.

glue		glue
glue		glue

3.   Using the box and the parrot we are going to learn about grammar. Using phrases, describe the parrot in relationship to the box.

          For example:

          Put the parrot <u>on</u> the <u>box</u>, and say "on the box."

          Try the following:

                    <u>above</u> the box   <u>over</u> the box
                    <u>in</u> the box   <u>around</u> the box
                    <u>to</u> the box.

          These phrases begin with a word that we call a preposition. Prepositions tell us the relationship between the parrot and the box. Think of several other phrases you can use to tell how the parrot relates to the box. [4a]

          Using two of these prepositional phrases write two complete sentences about the parrot and the box. What do you need to add to the phrase to make complete sentences?

4.   a. Read the passage to your teacher. Tell your teacher the following:

                    Who is the passage written about?
                    What events happened to them?

          List the words that tell you someone else wrote this story about the Wright boys.

          Rewrite the passage as though the Wright boys were writing about themselves. Which words can you use in place of the ones listed above?

      b. Take an oral spelling test.

5.   Take your final dictation. Check it with the model.

Teacher Helps:

2.   b.   Wright -- certain, or proper, name of people
Adams Street -- proper name of place
Cedar Rapids -- proper name of place
Iowa -- proper name of place
Cedar River -- proper name of place

              a comma

3.   Possible options: against, at, behind, below, inside, with, near, under.

         A subject (the bear) and a verb (what the bear <u>did</u> or <u>is</u>)

4.   The Wright boys: got acquainted with boys
                         got acquainted with city
                         see rapids in Cedar River
                         stand on bank
                         look at whirling water

The Wright boys, them, they, they, they,
We, us, we

Possible answer:
     We were friendly boys. It didn't take us long to get acquainted with the boys on Adams Street in Cedar Rapids, Iowa.

     We were getting acquainted with the city too. Today we had gone to see the rapids in the Cedar River. We were standing on the bank looking down at the whirling water.

It was Wilbur's act in the Wright and Johnston Circus that started the stilt craze in Richmond. By the time a week had passed, several boys had made stilts and were learning to use them.

Orville and Gansey were working on theirs. Wilbur was helping them. He showed them how to make foot rests and where to fasten them to the poles.

Reprint with permission of Macmillan Publishing Company from _Wilbur & Orville Wright_ by Augusta Stevenson. Copyright 1951, 1959 by the Bobs-Merrill Co., Inc.

1.   Take the first paragraph from dictation. Edit it with the model making corrections and circling all misspelled words. Copy the second paragraph on your paper.

2.   a.   Make a spelling list from your misspelled words. Discuss them with your teacher, looking for spelling patterns, areas of difficulty and other words that are spelled with the same patterns.

    b.   How many sentences are in the passage? What did you look for in the passage to count the sentences?

            Each sentence has a subject, or someone or something the sentence is written about. Tell your teacher the subject of each sentence found in the second paragraph. List these subjects on your paper numbered 1-3.

            What type of words are these subjects?

    c.   Look at these same sentences and tell your teacher what these subjects did in each one. List the one or two words after each subject on your paper. What type of words are in this second list?

d.   There are two types of verbs. One type is called an action verb. How do you think an "action verb" is described? If you can do it, it is an action verb. Act out the verbs:

run   are   help   show

jump   work   were   was

The words that you cannot act out are verbs too. Look at your list from 2.b. Where are these verbs found? They help the action verb work correctly in the sentences, and are called helping verbs.

e.   Make a list of three subjects and three verbs.

Example: **subject**   **verb**
         1.   The dog   jumped
         2.
         3.

Using your list, write three complete sentences.

Example: The dog jumped over the fence.

f.   Write each sentence again adding a helping verb before the action verb. (Sometimes the form of the action verb must change.) Example: The dog was jumping over the fence.

3.   Look at your sentences from yesterday. Circle the subject of each sentence in red and the verb or verbs in blue. Read the words that are left over to your teacher. Remembering the bear in the box, how many prepositional phrases did you use in these six sentences?

TEACHER'S NOTE: The game you will play today can be with two or three players. Directions will be given for two players, with alternative directions for three players found in [ ] brackets.

One person thinks of a subject and verb to be used as part of a sentence. For example: The cow ran. [One person thinks of a subject, example: The cow; and one person think of a verb, example: ran.]

The other person think of a prepositional phrase, example: on the roof. When everyone is ready everyone tells what he/she has thought of in the correct order: subject/ verb /prepositional phrase.

Example: The cow ran on the roof.

Some sentences are silly and some aren't. Play the game for several rounds, then rotate the parts and play again.

4. a. Using your dictionary, look up the word "helping." Which word do you have to look up to find "helping"?

Following the word help you find the entry for the word. What information do you see in the entry? Discuss with your teacher the parts of a dictionary entry.

Find the word "craze" in the dictionary. Discuss the entry and meaning of the word with your teacher.

    b. Take an oral spelling test.

5.   Take your final dictation on the paragraph.

Teacher Helps:

2.   b.   5
           Possible answers: Capital letters in front of sentences, periods at the end of sentences.

           Orville and Gansey
           Wilbur
           He

           Nouns or pronouns

     c.   were working
           was helping
           showed
           verbs (action and helping)

     d.   run, jump, work, help, show
           before the action verbs.

4.   help
           phonic spelling, part of speech, meanings, another part of speech, meanings for that, the word with prefixes and suffixes added.

Then came the great moment. They carried the glider to the top of the dune. Wilbur climbed on the lower wing and lay face-down. He grasped the bar that would move the wing tips. Orville began to loosen the ropes.

In spite of its load, the machine rose off the sand and up into the air, about eight feet. The brothers forgot their hours of hard work. The glider had lifted! Their ideas had been right, even if it did come down after a few seconds.

Reprint with permission of Macmillan Publishing Company from _Wilbur & Orville Wright_ by Augusta Stevenson. Copyright 1951, 1959 by the Bob-Merrill Co., Inc.

1.   Read the passage with your teacher. Take the second paragraph from dictation. Edit using the model.

2.   a.   List spelling words from any misspelled words on your dictation.

     b.   Using the first paragraph only, list the verbs of the subject used in each sentence. Look at the list and tell your teacher how three of them are alike.

          Write each word as it is before the -ed was added to the end. Make up a rule about adding -ed to the end of words. How does the -ed change the meaning of the word?

     c.   Write two other words on your list that are past tense.

          Which form of these words would you use for an event that was happening right now?

3.   Today you will rewrite the passage as if the events are happening right now. You can pretend you are standing in Kitty Hawk watching the whole scene. The first two sentences could read:

> The great moment has come. They are carrying the glider to the top of the dune.

Discuss the remainder of the passage with your teacher and then finish rewriting it.

4.   a.   This passage is taken from a biography written by Augusta Stevenson about Wilbur and Orville Wright. Since the story was written about them it is a biography of the Wright brothers. Look on your book shelves for several biographies of other people. Discuss how a biography is written with your teacher.

A biography is a story written by one person, about another person; it involves two people. An autobiography is a story written by a person about himself. If Wilbur Wright wrote a story about his life, that story would be an autobiography.

Pretend that Wilbur is writing this story himself about the events of the day. Circle the words that would need to be changed to make it an autobiography. Read the passage to your teacher changing these words to make it sound like Wilbur was writing the story.

    b.   Take an oral spelling test.

5.   Take the second paragraph from dictation.

Teacher Helps:

2. b. came
carried
climbed - lay
grasped - move
began - loosen

-ed added to the end

carry
climb
grasp

Possible answer: Add -ed to the end of the word. If the word ends in "y" and there is a consonant before the "y" change the "y" to "i" and add -ed.

-ed makes the word past tense, or an event that happened in the past

c. came, began
come, begin

4. Possible answers: They = we
Wilbur = I
He = I
The brothers = we
their = our
Their = Our

TEACHER'S NOTE: A trip to the library is suggested for the last day of this week. The purpose is to look at all the special reference materials that are available at the library only. Tell your librarian the nature of your student's project and request that a brief tour and explanation of the reference materials be given to your student.

You may want to use the Book Making Unit, Lesson 32 with this project.

1.   a.   These lessons are going to help you learn what research is, how we begin to do it and why we do research.

        Look up the word "research" in the dictionary. After reading the definition and discussing it with your teacher, write a definition of "research" in your own words.

    b.   There are many tools we can use in our investigation of a certain subject. Books we may use are an atlas, a dictionary or an encyclopedia. Research does not end with just reference books. Other tools could be newspapers, real books, pamphlets, brochures and even videos or TV shows. Another way to do research might involve talking with someone, or an interview. If our goal is to find and understand facts, can you think of any other ways to do this?

    c.   Gather any of these resources and decide what kind of information is in each.

2.   a.   The third thing we need to consider is why we do research. What do you want to do with the information? Here are some examples of research. Discuss them with your teacher and decide why you think the research is being done.

        1)   A lady calls ten different fabric stores asking what the price of denim cloth is at each one. (Find the lowest/highest price.)

2) Scientists measure similar tomato plants growing in two different fields with two different kinds of soil every week for four weeks. (Study the effects of soil on tomato plants.)

. 3) Your father asks for brochures, or descriptions of all the places of interest in a town you are going to visit. He also buys a newspaper from that town. (Planning a vacation)

b. These are some examples of research. It is not always something done by scientists and adults. It can also be done by children. Talk with your teacher and see if you can think of any times your parents have done research on something. Talk about what they did, how they did it and why they did it.

c. See if you can think of a time that you may have done research and didn't realize it. Discuss with your teacher what you did, how you did it and why.

TEACHER'S NOTE: Take two days to complete this activity.

3. a. Now that you have been introduced to what research is, some of the tools you can use and why you do it, let's look at our research project. Many upper elementary grade students follow courses of study to learn about the state where they live. We will also do that using many different research tools. Several weeks ago, you wrote to your state capital for information on your state. If you have received that information, get it out and look at it now.

b. As you look at different pieces of information you will be writing information down and keeping it in a folder. Pictures, drawings, maps and other things will also be included in your folder. With your teacher's help, get a folder especially for your work in this unit. A folder with pockets might be best for holding the information as you gather it.

c.   Here is your project. You are to get information on your state to give to a pretend family that is thinking of moving to your state. They really don't know anything about your state, so all the information you come across will be new to them. Think of this project in two ways: information you would provide to the parents and information you would give to the children in the family. The children in this family are the ages of you and your brothers and sisters.

d.   Discuss with your teacher what information the parents might need, want and enjoy (not just business facts, you can tell them about things that are of beauty or interest as well). Make a list of things you want to find out.

e.   Discuss with your teacher what information the children might want and enjoy. Make a list of things you want to tell them. You can assume that the children might be much like yourself.

4.   Visit your library and view the special reference materials available. Assistance from your librarian would be helpful in acquainting you with all the ways you can find information. Take your list of questions developed in Activity 3 and with your teacher's help, use the reference materials as well as checking out books that will provide useful information for your report. Be sure to ask your teacher to show you the card catalog and how it helps us find information.

NOTE TO STUDENT: You will now be given some small projects to carry out. Each one is to be included in your folder on your state. After each project, talk with your teacher about whether you think it helps you meet your goals of providing information to the new family. Also keep in mind that you want your report to look as nice as possible. You will be told later in this manual how to make your own books, so you may want to make this information into a book as well.

TEACHER'S OVERVIEW: For the next three weeks' lessons you will need to provide access to reference materials for your student such as an atlas, dictionary, and either a desk encyclopedia or a set. During this unit on research we will refer to encyclopedias; however, we do not want reading an excerpt from an encyclopedia to take the place of using many other books. Use the encyclopedia entries to get a limited amount of facts or to confirm what your student has read elsewhere. It may also be used to find other aspects of a topic to investigate in other sources. Encyclopedia entries are summaries of available information. When teaching a student how to do research we want to encourage him/her to use as many resources as possible. If the encyclopedia is the only thing read about a subject, only one publisher's point of view is being considered.

"Rewording encyclopedia articles is not an especially good way to learn to write, and it is a poor way to learn what research is."

Ruth Beechick
You CAN Teach Your Child Successfully p. 62

1.   a.   You will use several reference tools to learn about your state. Look at the atlas your teacher will provide for you. Find the map of your state. Look for the key, or box with symbols used on the map. Look at the symbols used and find out what they mean.

b.   Place a piece of plain white paper over the map of your state so that the whole map is covered. Use paper clips to secure the paper. Trace the map, including major features such as the capital, rivers, major cities and any other important landmarks. Talk with your teacher to determine what needs to be included on your map.

c.   Finish your tracing of your state map by filling in any remaining details after removing the paper from the map. Label your map. Consider outlining with markers or pens.

2. a. Every state in the United States has a state flag, a state bird and a state flower. Possible ways to find out what your state's flag, bird and flower are would be to look at your atlas, in the encyclopedia, or the material sent from your Chamber of Commerce.

   b. Choose at least two of these state symbols and make pictures of them either by tracing, drawing or cutting out pictures. Use an 8 1/2 x 11 inch piece of construction paper as a base to make a flag of your state. Choose the color construction paper that is the same as the majority of the flag. Cut and paste the other colors, symbols or letters on the base color. Take two days to complete these activities. These state symbols should be included in your report.

   c. It may be difficult to find out, but ask your teacher to help you find this information. Why do you think this bird and flower were chosen to represent your state? Why do you think your state flag has this design?

   d. Two kinds of maps that we can look at are political maps (which show things like cities, states and countries) and physical maps (which show land forms such as mountains, deserts, etc.) Discuss with your teacher why you think they are called political maps (because the boundaries are decided by governments) and physical maps. Also use your atlas to find an example of a political map and a physical map. An extra activity would be to try to find both kinds of maps of your state and trace both to include in your report.

3. a. Information about the people that live in a state is important. Look at the atlas and see if the number of people living in your state is given. This is called the population. Is any information given here about the kind of industry or work that is done by most of the people in your state? Does your state have special qualities that are part of its business; for example, a state located by large bodies of water probably has a large fishing or seafood industry. Many states grow things as part of their important industries. Record, or write this information down about your state.

b.   Check your encyclopedia or other books on your state to find out more about the main ways people in your state earn their living.

c.   Why do you think this information might be important to the new family moving to your state? Discuss your answer with your teacher.

4.   a.   When was your state founded, or begun? Who was your state founded by? When did your state join the United States of America? This information, which is your state's history may not seem like something you need to know, but it helps us understand how our state has grown, what problems have come up in the past and what it may need right now. Together with your teacher, read the information you received by mail and books obtained from the library, focusing on information about your state's history. Make notes on the things that seem most important to you.

b.   With your teacher's help, decide what you think are the most important facts about your state's history. Your teacher can assist you by writing down your thoughts and helping you edit, or make them the best you can. Thesauruses are books that have synonyms or words that have almost the same meaning as other words. As your sentences are written down, use a thesaurus to check at least two or three words to see if another word might tell better what you want to say. Your teacher will suggest words that you may want to look up in a thesaurus, or you may choose your own.

c.   After you and your teacher come up with at least two paragraphs (eight sentences) about your state's history, make a final copy that is your neatest work.

5.   a.   Now that we have looked at the past, what problems or struggles does your state face today? What resources or references do you think will help you answer this question? (Newspapers, TV news, interviews with people around town, books.) Together with your teacher look at several resources and choose one or two problems that your state seems to have and write a description of these problems. Several sentences will be adequate for each problem.

b. After looking at your state's history, does the past have any part in your state's problems today? For example, if your state had a big business that ended (like making cars) does your state now have a problem with people not having jobs? Include a clipping from any newspaper or magazine on one of your state's problems in your folder.

1. a. Having fun is an important part of family life. Make a list of places to see or things to do that are fun, and may be interesting or special about your state. For example, if you were new to Arizona you would probably want to see the Grand Canyon. This list will make up your suggestions to the new family of fun and interesting things to do.

    b. What information would be important to include so that our family could visit these places? (Where they are, prices for admission, type of attraction, etc.)

    c. Look up the word "brochure" and "pamphlet" in the dictionary. Tell your teacher in your own words what these words mean. Many places you can visit have brochures to tell people about them. Discuss with your teacher where you would be able to get these brochures the most easily. Include as many brochures as you can in your report. A folder with a pocket may be best for holding brochures.

2. Take the next two days to answer any remaining questions that you thought of at the beginning of our project. Have you provided all the information you think would be most important to the parents? Have you provided information of interest to the children?

3. a. We have completed all the research parts of our report. After you have found the answers to your questions, the research process is not yet finished. Now you must arrange and present your information neatly and in an organized way. Arrange the information you have written down in the order your assignments were given. If you would like to make any changes in the order, discuss them with your teacher.

    b. Look at the information you have gotten together. Look at each page with your teacher and decide if there are any pages that need to be recopied, or typed.

c.   We will now make a title page for your report. You need to include a name for your report (for example, <u>Living in Arizona</u>, or <u>Welcome to Arizona</u>) and your name as the author. Also include the date of your report.

d.   At the end of your report you need to include a bibliography, or list of books and resources that you used to write your report. Ask your teacher to help you find this information and arrange it in alphabetical order on a list. Here is a sample:

<u>Learning Language Arts Through Literature -- The Orange Book</u> by Debbie Strayer and Susan Simpson, Commonsense Press, Hawthorne, Florida, 1992.

A good order for this information is name of book (underlined), author, publisher, where it was published and the year it was published. The first letter of each title is what you use to put the resources in alphabetical order.

e.   When you have finished share your hard work with your family or others. If visitors come to your house from another state you may want to let them read your report.

INTRODUCTION TO TEACHER

This unit is designed to help you and your student gain a deep appreciation and understanding of poetry. By listening to, copying, illustrating, reciting, and creating poetry, your student will become acquainted with various aspects of punctuation, parts of speech, rhythm and rhyme involved in poetry. You will need at least one book of poems from your shelf or the library to use throughout the unit.

At the end of the unit your student will have completed his own book of poems, both selected from other authors and created himself. You may use the Book Making Unit for this poetry book, or follow the simple directions found in the poetry lesson. A presentation of this material will be planned by you and your student. Please keep this presentation as casual as is appropriate for you and your student. An important purpose of this unit is to have fun, laugh, and enjoy the learning.

1.   Look at your poetry book(s). What is the title of it? What do you know about this book from the title? With your teacher, look at the title page, table of contents and index in your book. Answer these questions as you look at your book.

a)   Who selected the poems in your book?

b)   Is there an illustrator for the book? If so, look at some of the pictures he/she drew for the poems.

c)   Is the table of contents divided into sections? What are the titles of these divisions? What do these titles tell you about the poems listed below them? Ask your teacher to show you how to use the table of contents. Find one or two poems found under a section of your choice.

d)   Using either the table of contents or the index, find and read, or ask your teacher to read to you, a poem about:

an animal
a season or
a sport

Find a poem written by:

Robert Browning
Robert Frost or
Walter de la More.

Look at the poem. Where is the author's name written? Find a poem with no author's name. What do you think it means when no author is listed?

2. Listen as your teacher reads this poem to you.

LONG, LONG AGO

> Winds through the olive trees
>   Softly did blow,
> Round little Bethlehem
>   Long, long ago.
>
> Sheep on the hillside lay
>   Whiter than snow;
> Shepherds were watching them,
>   Long, long ago.

What story did you think about when you heard the poem? Which words or phrases are used to make you think of the birth of Jesus when you hear the poem? List 2 or 3 other words or phrases the author could have used to make you think of Jesus' birth. Remember to number your list and put a period after the number. Example:

1.
2.

Copy the poem on your paper. Check the poem and be sure all your punctuation marks are included in your copy.

Look at the last line in each verse. Make up a rule about repeating a word in the same sentence. Tell the rule to your teacher. (10n)

3. Listen as your teacher reads this poem.

TO MARKET, TO MARKET

> To market, to market, to buy a fat pig,
> Home again, home again, jiggety jig.
> To market, to market, to buy a fat hog,
> Home again, home again, jiggety jog.

Read the poem. Read the poem aloud and clap your hands to the rhythm of each line -- there are four beats in the first one. How many are in the other three lines? What can you say about the rhythm of the lines in this poem?

Which lines rhyme in this poem? Read lines 1 and 2. Two lines of poetry that rhyme are called a couplet. Do you know the word "couple"? It means two. If I ask for a couple of cookies, I want 2 cookies. So a couplet is a couple of lines that rhyme. Let's write a couple of couplets. Copy the first line and the beginning of the second line below. Then fill in the rest of the second line to make a couplet. Try to make the rhythm match in one of these couplets.

> We looked around from shop to shop,
> Trying to find a _____.

> The balloon went up to the very top,
> I'm sad to say, it then _____.

4.   Today you will begin to make your own poetry book. You will need:

lined paper,
pencil,
crayons or colored pencils,
a pocket notebook or folder to keep your papers safe for the next
       three weeks, and
at least one poetry book.

Your book will be made up of poems you select, just like the editor of the book we looked at three days ago. You will select the poem, copy it and illustrate it. (We'll talk about that in a minute). Then you will file it in your notebook or folder for safe keeping.

Let's look at the couplets you wrote yesterday.

Read the first one to your teacher. In one word tell her what the couplet is written about. Now describe this word to her. Example: If your first couplet read:

> We looked around from shop to shop,
> Trying to find a big, red top.

That couplet is about a **top**. It is a **big** top. It is a **red** top. To illustrate that couplet you may draw a picture of a big, red top. If you do, then you are finished with the illustration.

What else is this couplet written about? (Shopping) Who went shopping? Where did they go shopping? That's up to you as the illustrator. You may draw yourself and your mom or dad shopping at a nearby shopping center or mall.

Begin your poetry book by copying one of your couplets on the paper. Be sure to check your spelling, commas and periods. Then illustrate the poem and color your illustration. Talk to your teacher about the layout of your pages.

TEACHER'S NOTE: Suggestions for the page layouts:
a) Use notebook paper to copy the poem and illustrate on that paper.
b) Use notebook paper to copy and plain white paper for illustrations. Glue one to the other.

5. Look in your poetry book and find a poem that contains one or more couplets. Copy and illustrate it for your book.

Find a poem that has more than two lines of rhyme. Copy and illustrate it for your book.

Read the poems to your teacher.

File them in your safe keeping folder.

Teacher Helps:

1.   The author is unknown for that poem. Many poems were handed down for generations without knowing who first composed the poem

2.   Jesus' Birth

                Possible words: star, manger, stable, the wisemen

                A comma is placed in a list of the same words.

3.   Four rhymes in each line.

                The rhythm in the lines of this poem are all the same.

                Lines 1 and 2; lines 3 and 4.

                Possible answer: big, red top.
                                      went pop.

1.   Listen as your teacher reads this poem.

THE BABY
George MacDonald

> Where did you come from, baby dear?
> Out of the everywhere into the here.
>
> Where did you get your eyes so blue?
> Out of the sky as I came through.
>
> What makes the light in them sparkle and spin?
> Some of the starry spikes left in.
>
> Where did you get that little tear?
> I found it waiting when I got here.
>
> What makes your forehead so smooth and high?
> A soft hand stroked it as I went by.

What do you hear in this poem that is different from the other ones you've heard in your lessons? This poem has a pattern to it. Each verse follows the same pattern: a question, then an answer.

Which lines rhyme in this poem? This is a series of couplets combined to make a long poem.

Copy the lines below and fill in the blanks to make your own pattern poem using questions.

> What's a big animal all covered with hair?
> It's nothing but a big black _____.
>
> How about an animal who chirps for a word?
> That's easy, it just a beautiful _____.

What sea animal will give you a stab?
The creepy, crawly little _____.

Could man's best friend be a hog?
Oh no, it's got to be a big _____ _____ .

What furry rodent does Mom want out of the house?
Why, our little friend the _____ _____ _____.

What would you like to see fried on a dish?
Oh, I'd like a _____ _____ _____.

Now read your newly written poems with your teacher. One person read the question and the other person read the response.

Illustrate your poem and file it in your folder.

2.   Look through your poetry book for a pattern poem. Remember not all of them have questions. Some use the same repeating line in a pattern, repeat lines throughout the poem or begin most lines with the same words.

TEACHER'S NOTE: These poems may be difficult to find. Here are suggestions you may give your child to look up in the book using the Table of Contents or the Index.

Wynken, Blynken & Nod -- Eugene Field
Hoosen Johnny -- Author Unknown
The Little Jumping Girls -- Kate Greenaway
Thanksgiving Day -- Lydia Maria Child
Slumber Song -- Louis V. Ledoux
Only One Mother -- George Cooper

3.   Listen as your teacher reads this poem.

THE SILENT SNAKE

The birds go fluttering in the air,
    The rabbits run and skip,
Brown squirrels race along the bough,
    The May-flies rise and dip;
But while these creatures play and leap,
    The silent snake goes creepy-creep!

The birdies sing and whistle loud,
    The busy insects hum,
The squirrels chat, the frogs say "Croak!"
    But the snake is always dumb.
With not a sound through grasses deep
    The silent snake goes creepy-creep!

Look at the poem. The first verse tells us how animals do things.
Tell your teacher how each animal's actions are described:

birds   squirrels

rabbits   May-flies   snake

The second verse tells us how animals make sounds. Tell your
teacher how each animal sounds:

birds   squirrels

insects   frogs   snake

Is the author saying the snake is stupid? Look up the word "dumb"
in you dictionary. Which definition do you think the author meant for
the word "dumb"? What is the title of the poem? There are two
reasons why he is called the silent snake. Can you name one of
them?

66

What kind of snake is he? A silent snake. The snake is described with the adjective "silent". Adjectives tell us what kind, what color, which one and how many about a person, place, animal or thing. (3a) Find an adjective to describe these animals:

the _____ bird (chirping, pretty, blue).

the _____ fish

the _____ bear

the _____ dog

the _____ turtle

the _____ snake

4.   Look in your poetry book Table of Contents or Index and find two poems about animals.

Copy and illustrate them for your book. File them for safe keeping.

5.   Read your selected poems from yesterday to your teacher. Talk to your teacher about the rhyme and rhythm of the poems. Do your poems use adjectives to describe the animals? Which adjectives are used in your poems?

Find one more animal poem to copy and illustrate.

Teacher Helps:

1.   Each verse begins with a question.

          Lines 1 & 2 rhyme, Lines 3 & 4 rhyme, etc.

          Possible answers:
   - bear
   - bird
   - crab
   - black dog
   - small, white mouse
   - nice, big fish

3.   Birds -- fluttering in the air
          Rabbits -- run and skip
          Squirrels -- race
          May-flies -- rise and dip
          Snake -- creepy-creep

          Birds -- sing and whistle loud
          Insects -- hum
          Squirrels -- chat
          Frogs -- croak
          Snake -- silent

          Moves silently, doesn't talk

          possible answers: quiet, blue, scaly fish
                        hairy, black, big bear
                        brown, happy, jumpy dog
                        slow, snapping, large turtle
                        quiet, long, beautiful snake

1. Listen as your teacher reads this poem to you.

> The Lord is my shepherd.
> I have everything I need.
> He gives me rest in green pastures.
> He leads me to calm water.
> Psalm 23

Have you heard this poem any other time in your life? Do you know where this poem is found? Use your Bible to read the entire poem.

If you have never memorized this psalm, do so this week. If you have already memorized it, find another psalm to memorize this week.

Here is a way to memorize a poem: read the first verse of the poem, then look away from the page and try to say as much as you can from that verse. Read the entire verse again and repeat the process until the whole verse is memorized. Then read the first two verses and look away to say as much of both verses as you can remember. In this way, you learn the whole poem rather than short phrases or words.

2   Copy and illustrate Psalm 23 for your poetry book. Work on your memorization.

3.   Listen as your teacher reads this psalm to you.

Give thanks to the Lord because he is good.
His love continues forever.

Give thanks to the God over all gods.
His love continues forever.

Give thanks to the Lord of all lords.
His love continues forever.

Only he can do great miracles.
His love continues forever.

With his wisdom he made the skies.
His love continues forever.

He spread out the earth on the seas.
His love continues forever.

He made the sun and the moon.
His love continues forever.

He made the sun to rule the day.
His love continues forever.

He made the moon and stars to rule the night.
His love continues forever.

Psalm 136

What type of poem do you call this psalm? What is the pattern line in this poem? Write two or three pattern lines that could be used in this psalm to replace "His love continues forever". Now read several verses with one of your pattern lines in place of the original one.

Work on your memorization of the psalm.

4.	Look in the book of Psalms for a pattern poem to copy and illustrate or copy and illustrate several verses from Psalm 136.

Recite as much of the psalm to your teacher as you have memorized by today. You and your teacher decide if you will recite your psalm to your family and if so, when you will recite it. Practice standing to recite, holding your hands still and looking at your audience.

5.	Using Psalms and Proverbs from the Bible find, copy and illustrate one passage for your book.

Work on your memorization.

Teacher Helps:

1.	Psalm 23

3.	Pattern Poem and/or Praise

His love continues forever.

Suggestions:	Our God is great and mighty

We love our Father God

We worship our Lord God

1.   Listen as your teacher reads this poem to you.

        THE MOON

> O, look at the moon
> > She is shining up there;
>
> O, Mother, she looks
> > Like a lamp in the air.
>
> Last week she was smaller
> > And shaped like a bow,
>
> But now she's grown bigger
> > And round like an O.

Now listen to the same idea written in prose.

A little girl was looking at the moon one night. She told her mother that the moon looked like a lamp in the sky. She also noted that the shape of the moon changed in a week's time.

What differences do you notice in the poem and the prose? Which one do you prefer to listen to, and why?

Read the poem to your teacher. When do you pause and/or take a breath while reading the poem? How does this help the sound of the poem?

Find another poem in your poetry book to read to your teacher. Copy and illustrate it, "The Moon", or any other poem you'd like to use in your selection of poems.

2. a. Listen as your teacher reads this poem to you.

THE VILLAGE BLACKSMITH
Henry Wadsworth Longfellow

Under a spreading chestnut-tree
The village smithy stands;
The smith, a mighty man is he,
With large and sinewy hands;
And the muscles of his brawny arms
Are strong as iron bands.

His hair is crisp, and black, and long,
His face is like the tan;
His brow is wet with honest sweat,
He earns whate'er he can,
And looks the whole world in the face,
For he owes not any man.

Using your Index or Table of Contents, try to find this poem in your book of poems. Ask your teacher to read the entire poem to you. Discuss the blacksmith with your teacher. How did he look? How did he act? A hard worker? A responsible person? Use parts of the poem to defend your answers.

b. The author uses many words to describe this man. Tell your teacher the describing words used to help us imagine the blacksmith's hands, arms, hair. (Use a dictionary if needed).

These words are adjectives describing nouns. (3a)

large hands
brawny arms
black hair

c. Another type of description is used to help us imagine the blacksmith's arms. It is a group of words, or phrase. Can you find it in the poem?

This phrase "strong as iron bands" compares two things. What are those two things? The phrase also uses the word "as" in the comparison, making it a simile.

Let's write some similes comparing a tree with several other objects.

The tree is as tall as _____.
The tree is as strong as _____.
The tree is as green as _____.

3.   Today, you may choose one of two activities to complete.

a)   You can make simile mobiles to hang from the ceiling or on the wall.

Think of an object, example: a flower. Draw the object in a large, simple way and cut it out as the top of your mobile. Then cut two or three rectangular pieces of paper to write your similes on and hang from your top piece. See the example below.

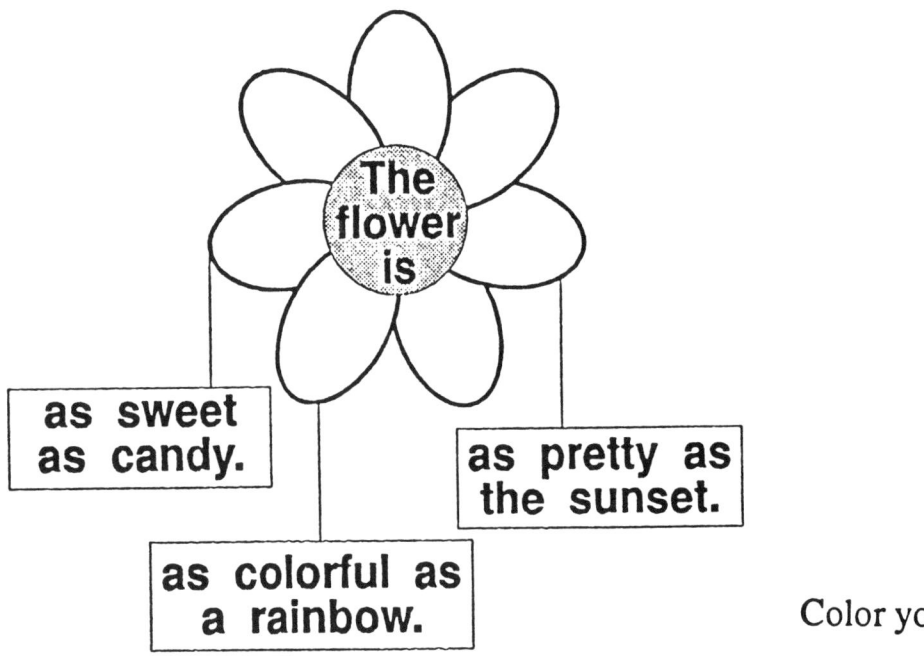

Color your mobile.

74

Make as many simile mobiles as you and your teacher think you have time to complete. Possible mobile ideas:

Fish:	as slimy as	Sun:	as hot as
	as big as		as big as
	as wet as		as shiny as

Clouds:	as soft as	Dog:	as fun as
	as fluffy as		as furry as
	as fun as		as brown as

b) Find one or two poems that use similes in them. Copy and illustrate for your selection of poems.

4. Do all poems have to rhyme? During the next two days you are going to write a new type of poem. Begin by thinking of an object you can easily draw; like a kite. Now think of things you could say about a kite.

Example: The kite flies high up in the sky.
The kite is gone -- bye-bye.

That's short and a little silly, but that's what happens to kites sometimes.

To write this poem, you draw the object. Example:

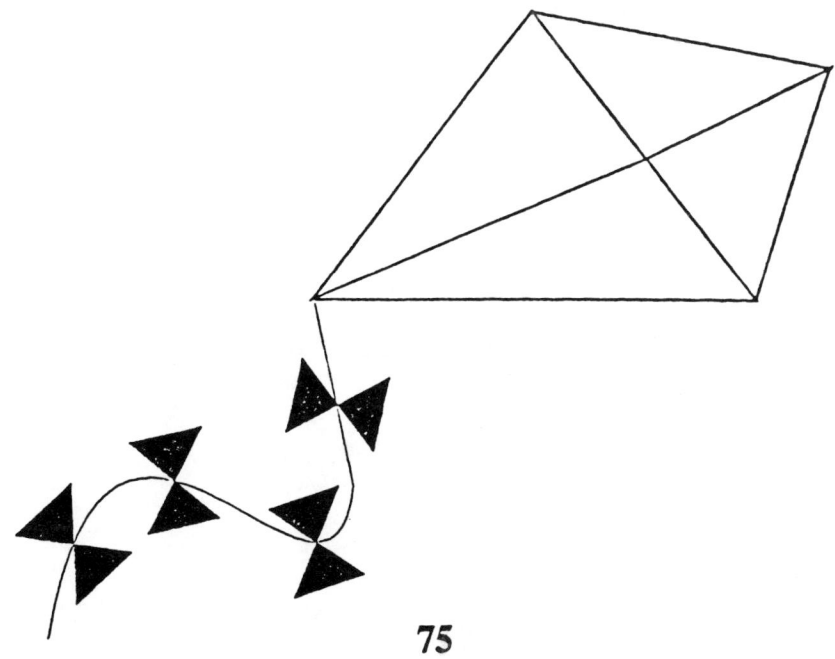

75

Now write the lines about the object on the lines of the drawing.

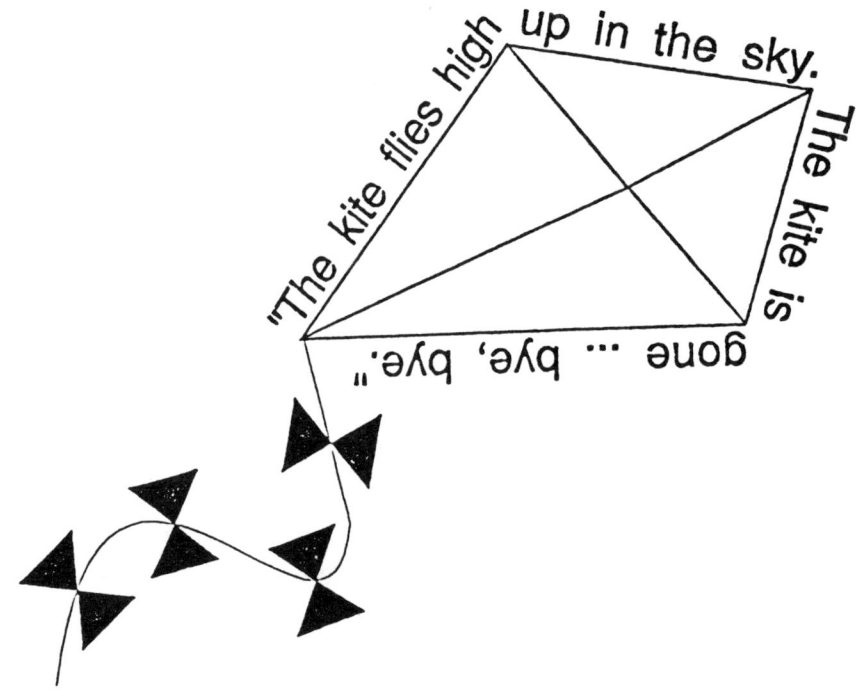

This is called a concrete poem, because the poem itself shows you what it is written about. With your teacher, think of several objects you could easily draw. List them on your paper. (Suggestions: boat, bird, flower, sun, star, car, square) Ask yourself, "What can I say about a _____?" With your teacher, write a line or two about two or three of the objects on the list using the question above to help you think ofideas.

5.   Using two of the objects from your list yesterday, write two concrete poems. If you can add color or more illustration to your poem, do so.

Teacher Helps:

1.   Possible answers:
                    Rhyme in the poem
                    Moon shape is described more in poem.
                    Rhythm in the poem.
                    Prose is like we talk everyday

            Pause and breathe at the end of every two lines to emphasize the
            rhyme.

2.   b.   Hands -- large, sinewy (strong, tough cord that joins muscles to bone,
            tendon)

            Arms - brawny (strong, muscular) strong

            Hair - crisp, black, long

      c.   "Strong as iron bands"
            His arms and iron bands.

            Possible answers: as tall as the sky, the clouds
                              as strong as the wind, the blacksmith
                              as green as the grass, my daddy's car

1. Listen as your teacher reads this poem to you.

> Whisky Frisky,
> Hippity hop,
> Up he goes
> To the tree top!
>
> Whirly, twirly,
> Round and round,
> Down he scampers
> To the ground.

What do you think this poem is written to describe? The name of the poem is "The Squirrel" and the author is unknown.

Read the poem again with your teacher and listen for describing words. Tell your teacher the four describing words used for the squirrel.

Read it again and look for words that tell the actions of the squirrel. Tell your teacher the action words.

Today you will begin work on a special type of poem that uses describing words and action words. Begin by thinking of a subject, example: apple.

On your paper write the word "apple" on line one. Discuss with your teacher how an apple looks, feels, tastes and write down two words that describe the apple on line 2. Put a comma between these two words. Example:

> Line 1 -- apple
> Line 2 -- red, juicy

Discuss with your teacher what the apple can do or what we do with the apple -- think of action words. List 3 action words, with commas between them on line three.

Line 3 -- bite, crunch, munch

Now discuss with your teacher what you like about the apple or what you don't like about it. Use a four word phrase in Line 4 to tell how you feel about the apple, with no commas used now.

Line 4 -- so good to eat

For Line 5, you need to find a word that is similar to the word used in Line 1. You may use your thesaurus to find a synonym for the word in Line 1. Example:

Line 5 -- Fruit

Our poem now looks like this:

apple
red, juicy
bite, crunch, munch
so good to eat
fruit

This poem is called a cinquain. It has 5 lines, as follows:

Line 1 --   one word, subject or idea
Line 2 --   two words that describe the subject
Line 3 --   three words that tell action of or about the subject
Line 4 --   four words that tell your reaction to the subject
Line 5 --   one word that is a synonym or similar to the subject

2.   Write one or two cinquain poems. Possible subjects: animals, people, food or plants

3.   Listen as your teacher reads this poem to you.

THERE WAS AN OLD MAN WHO SAID "DO"

There was an old man who said "Do
Tell me how I should add two and two?
   I think more and more
   That it makes about four --
But I fear that is almost too few."

Read the poem with your teacher. There are five lines in this poem. Which lines rhyme? How many accented phrases are there in each line? This type of poem is called a limerick.

Writing limericks can be difficult, so we are going to write one together. We need three rhyming words for lines 1, 2 and 5. List several words that rhyme with light.

Now we need two rhyming words for lines 3 and 4. List words that rhyme with go.

For our poem we will use:

   light   go   night   show   might

Copy this poem, complete it and illustrate for your selection of poems.

The man from Brazil had a light

That shone throughout the whole _____.

So off he'd ____

To the new puppet _____

Then run home with all of ____ _____.

4.   Write a limerick and illustrate it OR find a limerick in your poetry book to copy and illustrate for your selection of poetry.

Optional: Another type of poetry you may want to write is called haiku (hi-ku). It is a Japanese poem with 3 lines that do not rhyme. But each line has a certain number of syllables in it.

Line 1 - five syllables
Line 2 - seven syllables
Line 3 - five syllables

The number of words does not matter, only the number of syllables. Example:

1 2 3 4 5
The sun/ny sum/mer
1 2 3 4 5 6 7
Full of fun, play and sun/shine
1 2 3 4 5
My fav/or/ite time

Write one or two haiku poems.

5.   Discuss with your teacher the following:

a)   How many more poems are needed for your poetry selections?

TEACHER'S NOTE: Determine how worthwhile this is for your child to continue copying or creating poetry, then guide him to more or fewer poems to include.

b)   What type of poems are needed?

TEACHER'S NOTE: Try to round out the type of poems included in his selections. Make up a list of other titles, authors or subjects to include in the selections. Encourage him to use the index or table of contents to find these poems.

c)   How are you going to bind and cover your selection of poems?

TEACHER'S NOTE: Suggestions: 1) simple construction paper cover with the pages stapled on the side, 2) a paper folder to hold papers. Help your child make the title page and illustrated cover with title, 3) refer to the Book Making Unit.

d)   What type of a presentation will be given to your family?

Suggestions:
          -- reading from your selections
          -- reciting one or more of your poems
          -- passing the selection book around for everyone to see

Teacher Helps:

1.   squirrel

          whisky, frisky, whirly, twirly

          hop, goes, scampers

3.   lines 1, 2 & 5 -- 3 accented syllables

          lines 3 & 4 -- 2 accented syllables

          Possible answers: night, might, bright

                              show, blow, so

          night
          go
          show
          his might

1.   Spend the next four - six days completing your poetry selection book and preparing for your presentation. Use the following checklist to help you:

        ____ all poems copied and illustrated

        ____ table of contents completed

        ____ title page completed

        ____ index made (optional)

        ____ cover illustrated

        ____ book bound and completed

        ____ presentation prepared

Matt stood at the edge of the clearing for some time after his father had gone out of sight among the trees. There was just a chance that his father might turn back, that perhaps he had forgotten something or had some last word of advice. This was one time Matt reckoned he wouldn't mind the advice, no matter how many times he had heard it before. But finally he had to admit that this was not going to happen. His father had really gone. He was alone, with miles of wilderness stretching on every side.

1.   Read the passage with your teacher. Take the first two sentences from dictation. Edit from the model.

2.   a.   Make your spelling word list from the misspelled words. Discuss the spelling patterns of each word and why each one was misspelled. Tell your teacher one to two words with the same spelling pattern as your words.

      b.   Number your paper 1-8. Read silently through the passage and as you read, write any word you find that has letters added to the end of it.

      Example: jump-ing.

      In this word, the letters "ing" have been added to the word jump.

      In your list, circle all the words as they are before the letters were added. These are the base words. Tell your teacher the letters, or suffixes that were added to each base word.

TEACHER'S NOTE: Point out that in forgotten, only <u>en</u> is the suffix. Use the optional lesson below if needed.

Using a book from your shelf, find a word with each of these suffixes added to it and show it to your teacher.

c. OPTIONAL: Look at each base word. How were any of them changed when the suffix was added? Look at these words: jumping, running, hopping, looking

In two of these words, the last consonant is doubled before the suffix is added. Which words are they, and how are they alike? Can you make up a rule about adding suffixes to base words? Does the word *forgotten* follow this rule?

3. a. Read this with your teacher.

Matt stood for some time after his father had gone. There was a chance that his father might turn back. Finally he had to admit his father was gone. He was alone.

Reread the passage. Do they both contain the same information? Look at the first sentence of each paragraph. They both tell us that Matt stood for awhile after his father had gone. What type of information is added in the passage sentence? Look for any other types of information that is given in the passage. How does it enhance the story? Which paragraph do you like best?

b. Read this sentence: The dog ran.

What does that sentence tell you? Talk to your teacher about filling out the sentence using questions such as:

What kind of dog? (color, size, age)
Where did he run?
How did he run?
When did he run?

After your discussion, write a new sentence giving the same information, but filled out.

> Example: Yesterday, the big, brown dog ran quickly through the garden.

"Fill out" one of these sentences:

| The cat jumped. | The boy sat. |
| Mom helped me. | This book is good. |

4.   a.   Read the first three sentences to your teacher. Write two to three sentences describing how Matt felt during this time.

   Read the last three sentences to your teacher. What event happened to make the feeling different from the first section of the passage?

   b.   Take an oral spelling test.

5.   Take the first two sentences from dictation. Correct with the model.

Teacher Helps:

2.   b.   clear - ing
   tree - s
   forgot - ten
   reckon - ed
   time - s
   final - ly
   mile - s
   stretch - ing

   forgotten - a **t** was added before the **en.**

      c.   running, hopping -- They both have a short vowel before the last consonant.

   If a one syallabe word ends in a consonant with a short vowel in front of it, you must add the same consonant again before you add the suffix.

   When a two or more syllable word ends in this way and is accented on the last syllable, the rule applies.

3.   a.   Yes

   Where he stood, where his father had gone.

   Possible answers: - Why his father may turn back.
                       - How Matt longed for him to turn back
                       - Matt's admittance that what he wanted would not happen.
                       - Matt was in the middle of the wilderness.

   It enhances the story by helping us see the picture of a boy alone in the woods and gives us help in understanding Matt's feelings.

3.   b.   The dog ran.

4.   a.   Matt had to admit his father was not coming back. He was alone.

He turned and looked back at the log house. It was a fair house, he thought; his mother would have no cause to be ashamed of it. He had helped to build every inch of it. He had helped to cut down the spruce trees and haul the logs and square and notch them. He had stood at one end of every log and raised it, one on top of the other, fitting the notched ends together as snugly as though they had grown that way. **He had climbed the roof to fasten down the cedar splint with long poles, and dragged up pine boughs to cover them. Behind the cabin were the mounds of corn he had helped to plant, the green blades already shooting up, and the pumpkin vines just showing between the stumps of trees.**

From The Sign of the Beaver by Elizabeth George Speare. Copyright (c) 1983 by Elizabeth George Speare. Reprinted by permission of Houghton Mifflin Co. All rights reserved.

1.   Read the passage with your teacher. Take the last two sentences from dictation. Edit with the model.

2. a.   Make your spelling word list.

     b.   Copy the first sentence in the passage. Underline the subject and circle the two action verbs. Which word connects these two verbs? This connecting word for the action verbs is called a conjunction.

     c.   Find and circle with a blue pencil (or point out to your teacher) the other conjunctions in this passage. Tell your teacher the words or phrases these conjunctions connect in each sentence.

3. a. Look at the sentence below:

   Matt watched his father go through the trees.

   Is this a complete sentence? How do you know?

   Complete sentences contain two parts: [5g]
       the subject: who or what the sentence is about - *Matt*
       the predicate: that tells something about the subject - *watched his father . . . .*

   b. What types of words do you think are used in the subject of a sentence? [5h] Discuss the subject of the sentence with your teacher again.

   What type of word must be included in the predicate of the sentence? [5j]

   Tell your teacher three complete sentences. Write one of these complete sentences. Fill it in with: who, when, where, how many, and what kind of words if it is needed.

4. Read the passage from last week and the one from this week. Tell your teacher the story of Matt from these passages. Talk to your teacher about what you think may have happened before this part of the story.

   Answer questions, such as:

   Why did Matt and his father build the house?
   Where is Matt?
   Why did his father leave him?
   Where is his father going?

   Write three or four sentences telling what you think happened before Matt's father left.

5. Take the last two sentences from dictation.

Teacher Helps:

2. b. He turned looked
        and

    c. cut down the spruce trees
        haul the logs
        square notch them

        had stood at one end of every log
        raised it

        had climbed ...
        dragged up ...

        green blades shooting up
        the pumpkin vines.

3. a. Yes -- It includes a subject - Matt - and tells something about the
        subject.

    b. Nouns or pronouns
        Verbs -- action or helping (linking)

He was sitting on the flat stone that served as a doorstep, waiting for his supper to cook. The late sun slanted in long yellow bars across the clearing. The forest beyond was already in shadow. **Matt was feeling well pleased with his day. That morning he had shot a rabbit. He had skinned it carefully, stretching the fur against the cabin wall to dry.**

1.   Read the passage with your teacher. Copy the passage on your paper. With your teacher, make a spelling list from the last three sentences.

2.   a.   Using your spelling words, find the spelling pattern for each word. Discuss with your teacher the possible problems in spelling each word.

      b.   With a red pencil, circle each name of a person, place or thing, or a noun. With a blue pencil, circle every word that describes a noun. Words that describe, or tell how many, which one, what kind of about the person, place or thing, are called adjectives. How do adjectives help a sentence?

      c.   Look at your passage again and circle in green the word or words that answer these questions. In sentence #4, **how** is Matt feeling about his day? In sentence #5, **when** did he shoot the rabbit? In sentence #6, **how** did he skin the rabbit? The word or words you gave answered the questions: how, when and where. Were they all single word answers or phrases? These are adverbs or adverbial phrases.

d. Copy the sentence below and circle the noun in red, the adjective in blue, the verb in yellow and the adverb in green. Discuss this with your teacher before you begin.

Today, the big, black cat jumped carefully from the tree.

(OPTIONAL: What type of word begins the adverb phrase? [preposition])

3. a. Read the first sentence in the passage to your teacher. The subject of the sentence is "He". What word shows the action of the subject? That is a verb in the predicate. There is another verb in the predicate that helps the verb "sitting". Can you find it? The verb in this sentence is "was sitting". Helping verbs are words such as:

is	are	was	were	
has	have	had	should	
be	being	might	could	[2b]

Read each sentence in the passage and tell your teacher what the verb or verbs are in it. If there is a helping verb, tell her which one is helping.

4. Write a journal entry for Matt's day. Include a date and three or four sentences describing a part of Matt's day. Talk to your teacher about a realistic made-up date and how you will write your sentences.

5. Take the last two sentences from dictation.

Teacher Helps

2.   b.   *(flat)* stone, doorstep, supper
               (late) sun, *(long yellow)* bars, clearing
               forest, shadow
               Matt, day
               morning, rabbit
               fur, *(cabin)* wall

               Adjectives give us more details about something or someone. They help us see the picture more clearly.

     c.   #4 How? Well pleased
               #5 When? That morning
               #6 How? carefully

               Single words and phrases

     d.   Noun - cat, tree
               Adjectives - big, black
               Verb - jumped
               Adverbs - carefully, Today
                     (from the tree)

3.   sitting (waiting)
           was

           slanted
           was
           was (helper) feeling
           had (helper) shot
           had (helper) skinned   (although stretching is a verb, it refers to "the fur" not "He", the subject of this sentence.)

           were (helper) boiling

TEACHER'S NOTE: This five to six week unit will involve your student in recording information about his/her life. A camera will be very helpful in this process. If one is not available, please encourage your student to draw pictures in place of the photographs.

1.   a.   There are several types of journals.

      b.   One kind of journal entry tells about several events, or things that have happened. Here is an example:

> Summer was a busy time. My brother
> went to baseball camp. My cousin
> came and spent a week with us. Our
> family drove to Grandma's. On the
> way we went camping. It was fun.

The topic of summer is a very large topic and several events were described that may not have happened very close together.

      c.   What do most of these sentences tell about? (people & events) Were there many thoughts or feelings described?

      d.   Together with your teacher discuss events or several things that have happened that you would like to describe. Write at least three or four sentences. Here are some possible topics:

> a holiday
> a birthday
> a season (fall, etc)
> a school year
> a summer

After you write your sentences, discuss them with your teacher and make any changes you feel are needed.

2. a. Sometimes journal entries can be very specific and have more details. Here is an example:

Monday, May 18, 1992

Today I finished Lesson 26 in language arts. We worked on multiplication and division with rods and I did 10 written problems. Our Bible story was about how we should be patient and keep trying. I looked up "patient" in the dictionary. After lunch, Mom read a book out loud to us about knights and armor.

The specific event described here was a day of school. A business man might write down what he sold in a day, or a coach might write down how his team did in a game.

b. Together with your teacher, discuss a specific event that you can describe. If no other event comes to mind, describe a day of school.

c. After composing, or making up a couple of sentences orally, write them down. Read them with your teacher and make any needed changes.

3. a. Another kind of journal entry is writing down your thoughts or feelings. This is sometimes hard for people. Here is an example:

My first baseball game as a pitcher is over. I was scared when I walked out to the mound. Everything happened very fast. One kid had a great hit but we got them out. Dad and the coach said I did well. It felt good to be a pitcher.

b. Does the writer tell about things that happened? Does he/she tell about feelings? Think of an event or a subject that you can tell your thoughts or feelings about.

c. After discussing them with your teacher, write at least four sentences that describe your thoughts and feelings about an event or topic.

d. Reread your sentences with your teacher and make any needed corrections or changes.

4. a. Look over the three samples and journal entries you wrote for the past week. Tell your teacher what differences you see between them.

b. Choose one of the types of journal entries we have looked at and write another one following that same style.

c. You may want to start helping your teacher keep a record of your school work. If you don't want to keep track of all of it, choose a subject (such as math) or a unit (such as the ocean) and keep a written record of the work you did and the date you did it.

5. a. When you write, it needs to be clear and understandable to another person. Think of a simple activity that is done around your home. Without telling your teacher what it is, write down directions on how to do that activity from beginning to end. Some possible activities are making a bed, making a sandwich, playing a game, putting a toy together, etc.

b. Give the directions to your teacher. Ask your teacher to read and follow the directions. Was he/she able to do the activity? Do you need to make any changes?

c. If any changes were made, give the directions to another person and ask him to follow them. As you can see, it is very important to give people enough clear information when you want them to understand something.

d. You may want to try this again with a more complicated activity. Try to write directions in a simple way so that anyone could follow them.

1.   Have you heard of a time capsule? It is something that is written and compiled to tell about life today, buried in the ground to be found many years from now by others who can learn about our lives. If a time capsule buried 100 years ago was found today, we could learn about the daily lives of the western pioneers or the building of the railroads, and many other things about people's life so long ago.

          These next few weeks you will be working on creating a time capsule about you and your family's life. Whether you bury it or not, you will want to keep it in a safe place to be read years from now.

          Using poster board or construction paper, make a sign for your room or play area. You can write your name on it, (Ex: Michael's Room) or another appropriate name or saying on the sign. Decorate it with pictures or designs. Color or paint it.

2.   Choose a place that is important to you: your room or play area. Draw a map of the area, labeling all the important things included in that area.

                    Example: for your bedroom, include the furniture, baseball glove, bat, books, etc.

          TEACHER'S NOTE: This activity can be expanded to include measuring the walls and drawing the map to scale. (1 ft. = 1 in.).

3.   Using one piece of paper for each person in your family, write their name at the top of the paper. Using a ruler, make two columns on the paper. Label one column "Who is He or She", the other column, "What Does He or She Do."

Under the first column (Who is He/She), write descriptive phrases of this person. Write about how he looks, how he acts, and how he treats other people. Under the second column (What He/She Does), write phrases that tell what this person does throughout a normal day, what she likes to do for fun, and what she does in church or other groups.

Complete two or three of these pages today.

TEACHER'S NOTE: Spend plenty of time discussing these sheets with your student before he begins to write them.

4.   Continue work on your family sheets. Begin to take pictures of each family member. You may want to take one of your brother building with his favorite blocks or mom reading to the children. You decide the type of picture you need for each person.

5.   Continue your family sheets and picture taking.

Draw a map of your house and yard. Label each room and area.

Today begins journal writing about your life. There is no need to write about everything in your day, but choose one event and describe it, including important details and your feelings about what happened.

The entry will begin with the date and contain four - eight sentences about the event.

            Example: April 30, 1992 --

Each entry needs to be on a separate piece of paper.

During this time, take pictures of places and people that are an important part of your life. You may want to take a picture that goes along with your journal entry.

By mid to late week your picture taking needs to be completed so they can be developed.

August 16, 1992

Dear Aunt Mary,

Today our family went to the beach. This beach is fun to explore during low tide. There are many tide pools with crabs, shellfish, and minnows. We even found a starfish.

There are also big rocks to climb and waves to play in at this beach. Maybe we can go there when you visit us this fall.

Love,

Jana

1. a. Read this letter with your teacher. Talk to your teacher about the letter. Who is it written to, when was it written and who is writing it?

    b. What kind of information is found in this letter? Do you think Aunt Mary will enjoy reading this letter? Why do you think this? By writing letters, we share our lives with others who are not with us.

    c. Make a list of people you think would enjoy receiving a letter from you. You will not be asked to write to each one, so you can make the list as long as you can make it. Number your paper, with a period after the number, and write the person's name after the period.

        Example:
                    1.   Uncle Don
                    2.   Aaron

2. a. Using your list that was made yesterday, choose one person to write a letter. Look at the sample letter in our lesson. Where do you write the date on your paper? The greeting begins:

"Dear ___".

Where is that written and what punctuation mark follows the name? [12a &b]

b. The body of the letter gives all the information. How does the body of the letter begin? [12c]

c. The closing of the letter says goodbye to the reader. In our sample we use "Love". Where is that written on the paper? What other closing words can you use in your letter? What punctuation mark follows the closing? [12d] What follows the closing? [12e]

Talk to your teacher about the letter you want to write to the person you have chosen. Begin writing your letter.

3. a. Finish writing your letter. Ask your teacher to proofread it for spelling, capitals, and punctuation. Discuss any changes that need to be made on the letter.

b. Find an envelope for your letter. Ask your teacher to show you how to address the envelope, and where to put the stamp. [12i]

Fold your letter, put it in the envelope and mail it.

4. Choose another person from your list and write him a letter OR choose one member of your family and write him/her a letter. If you write to a family member, tell him/her about something you have done that he was not included in, or your thoughts and feelings about something in your life.

Example: You could write to Dad about a project in school. You could write to your brother about how much you like playing catch with him.

Whether you mail the letter or leave it on someone's pillow, put it in an envelope.

5.   Many people write their prayers in the form of a letter to God. Of course, there's no envelope to fill out for this type of letter. For many people, writing down their prayers helps them express themselves more fully.

Talk to your teacher about the letter you will write today. You may write one to a relative on your list, to a family member about your thoughts, or your prayers to God.

Complete the letter and mail it if necessary.

Teacher Helps:

1.   Possible answers: - Where the family went on a trip.
                                    - Details about the beach.
                                    - Invitation for Aunt Mary to go to the beach.

2.   a.   Date - top right section

                Greeting - left side, comma

      b.   Body - indented

      c.   Closing - after the body and indented under the date

                Sincerely   Your friend
                comma
                The writer's name

3.   Return
                Address

                       Mailing Address
                          Zip Code

The next week you will complete two projects. With your teacher, discuss a plan to use your daily time wisely. A daily checklist may be helpful or goal setting for mid-week and the end of the week.

PROJECT #1: Look at your photographs. Decide how you want to present them in a photo album. Example: family members first, house, yard, friends OR events on Monday, Tuesday, etc. OR things I like to do, friends I like to be with, etc.

Mount the pictures on construction paper, write a sentence or two about each picture either on the construction paper or on notebook paper to be glued under the photograph.

PROJECT #2: Using your family sheets that were made two weeks ago, an interview with each family member and your own observations, write about each family member. Using a separate piece of paper for each person, write four - eight sentences about a typical day from your family member's point of view. Include feelings the person may have and an event that you know about. It's like a journal entry for that person. Use "I" as you write to mean that family member.

Example: When you are writing from Dad's point of view it may
            sound like this:
            After breakfast, I dressed for work. Leaving the family
            everyday is hard.

At the completion of these projects, decide how you want to perserve them. You can bind the photo pages and journal pages in separate books using the book making unit, or the poetry book ideas. You can find a box to decorate and keep all your materials safely in that for years to come. Discuss this with your teacher and complete the unit.

Before Uncle Alfred could answer, there arose the most tremendous ruckus: a big, booming roar. HAR-ROOMF! Easily, the most thrilling and frightening noise Anabelle had ever heard. And the loudest. HAR-ROOMF! HAR-ROOMF! HAR-R-R-ROO-MM-FF!

It sounded like ... like ... the young hedgehog did not know *what* it sounded like. She had never heard anything *like* it before in her short life.

"What was that?" Anabelle asked, turning wide eyes to the far bank of the canal. The big, booming noise was coming from across the water.

Passages taken from The Tale of Annabelle Hedgehog are copyright 1990 by Stephen Lawhead. Published by Lion Publishing, Baravia, Illinois. Used by permission.

1. Read the last paragraph with your teacher. Take it from dictation. Edit from the model and make corrections.

2. a. Make your spelling list and discuss it with your teacher. Read the entire paragraph with your teacher. Tell your teacher which words are written in an unusual manner.

   b. When reading a story, we cannot hear sound like on a tape or video. To communicate sound, the author has used letters to make a sound word. Find that word and pronounce it with your teacher. The author has used familiar letter combinations or words in this made up word to help us pronounce it. Why do you think it is written in all capitals? What other thing is used to do this?

   c. The author uses one word twice with dots or periods to separate them. How does this add to the story?

d. Why do you think two other words are written in italics?
Read the paragraph to your teacher using expression and emphasis in your voice.

3. a. In the beginning of our paragraph, Uncle Alfred is about to answer a question. Before he can do that, there is a noise heard. Tell your teacher what kind of noise was heard.

Anabelle is the hedgehog who is hearing this noise. She heard many loud noises in her life. Of all the noises she has ever heard, how does this one compare with all the others?

She may have heard a car before now. That noise was:
    tremendous
    thrilling
    frightening and
    loud

She may have heard a bulldozer before now. That noise was:
    more tremendous than the car
    more thrilling than the car
    more frightening than the car and
        louder than the car

But this noise is:
    the most tremendous,
    the most thrilling
    the most frightening and
    the loudest of them all

We just compared Anabelle's description of three noises she has ever heard.

car	bulldozer	new noise
tremendous	more tremendous	most tremendous
thrilling	more thrilling	most thrilling
frightening	more frightening	most frightening
loud	louder	loudest

b.   This shows two ways to show comparison. Discuss with your teacher how you change words to compare two items. How do you change words to compare three or more items? [3e]

c.   Some words must be changed completely to compare. [3f] Use these words in a complete sentence to compare two items. Use them again to compare three or more items.

        bad   good   many

4.   a.   Can you think of another word that means the same as or similar to the word "big"? Words like: "huge" and "large" are synonyms of the word "big". They mean the same as or similar to the word big. A thesaurus is a book of synonyms. If you have a thesaurus, use it to find synonyms for the adjectives we found in our passage yesterday. Rewrite the first paragraph of passage replacing some of the adjectives with synonyms.

      b.   Take an oral spelling test.

5.   Take the last paragraph from dictation.

Teacher Helps:

2. a.   HAR-ROOMF

    b.   HAR-ROOMF (all capitals, made up word)

    c.   like...like... (periods after words, the word is repeated)
         what, like (italics)
         To show the force of the sound. The word ends in an exclamation point.
         It helps us feel or experience with words the confusion of the hedgehog.

    d.   Italics show emphasis

3. a.   Possible answers: most tremendous ruckus
                          big, booming roar
                          the most thrilling and frightening noise
                          the loudest noise

         the most tremendous
         the most thrilling and frightening
         loudest

    b.   Compare two items -- add more before the adjective or add er to the end.

         Compare three or more items -- add most before the adjective or add est to the end.

    c.   bad   worse   worst
         good   better   best
         many   more   most

4. a.   Possible answers: huge, large

"It means," replied the elder hedgehog, "that you simply put yourself in the dog's place, and think how you would like someone to behave towards you."

"But I don't know the first thing about being a dog," young Anabelle pointed out. "I don't know the first thing about anything, really."

1.   a.   Read the passage with your teacher. What is the most tremendous noise that Anabelle heard in our last passage? Why do you think she says the last line? Take the passage from dictation. Edit with the model.

2.   Make your spelling list from the misspelled words. Discuss with your teacher.

Find the words "dog" and "dog's" in the passage. Tell your teacher what word is written before dog. These words, **a**, **an**, and **the**, are special types of adjectives called articles. [3b]

The first time dog is used in the passage, the elder hedgehog is talking to Anabelle about the dog who has been barking. It is a very specific dog -- the dog.

The second time dog is used, Anabelle is talking about being a dog, or any dog. [3b]

If your teacher tells you to go to the shelf and get a book, which one will you get? Any book you want to get, because all she said was to get a book. Which one will you get, if she says to get the book? You may need more information to get the book she wants you to get from the shelf.

Find a book, any book, from your shelf and locate articles in it. Tell your teacher if they are describing specific items.

3.   Look at the passage.   Answer these questions about it with your teacher.

1.   How many characters are talking in the passage?
2.   How many paragraphs are there in the passage?
3.   What rule can you make up about paragraphs and writing what characters are saying, or dialogue?
4.   When you split the words said with who said them, how do you use commas?
5.   Where do you put a comma when you do not split the words said?

4.   Review your rules and observations about dialogue writing from yesterday. Using characters from a story or real people in your life, write a dialogue of two or three paragraphs.

Double check the paper using what you learned yesterday.

Take an oral spelling test.

5.   Take the passage from dictation or add to your dialogue writing from yesterday.

Teacher Helps:

1.   a dog's bark

        Possible answer: It shows her frustration with the problem, or it shows how inadequate she feels to deal with the problem.

2.   the, a

3.
    1.   2
    2.   2
    3.   Every time a new character begins to talk, a new paragraph is made in the writing.
    4.   Put a comma before the closing quotation mark, after the name of the person who talked and before the quotations open again.
    5.   Put a comma after the last word spoken and before the closing quotation marks.

"It's very simple," Herkimer told her. "To turn an enemy into a friend, all you have to do is love him."

"Love him? Are you sure? That doesn't sound easy at all. That sounds terribly difficult to me."

"Oh, it is difficult," Herkimer agreed. "Probably one of the most difficult things in the world. But I said it was simple, not easy."

Passages taken from The Tale of Annabelle Hedgehog are copyright 1990 by Stephen Lawhead. Published by Lion Publishing, Baravia, Illinois. Used by permission.

1. Read the passage with your teacher. Copy the passage on your paper. Check your copy with the model and make any corrections needed.

2. a. Make a spelling list of difficult words from the first two paragraphs. Discuss them with your teacher.

    b. Discuss the passage with your teacher. Who do you think the enemy is in this passage?

In this story, Anabelle has told the other animals that she will take care of the dog problem. Last week we heard some advice given to her by the elder hedgehog. In this passage, Herkimer is giving her more advice. What advice does he give her?

Herkimer gives her advice that he calls "simple", but not "easy." How can something be simple but not easy? Use your dictionary to look up the meaning of each word. There are several definitions for simple. Which one best suits the use in this paragraph? Which one best suits the use of the word "easy" in this paragraph? How is Herkimer's advice simple but not easy?

3.   Today you will begin writing a story that you create. Before you begin, discuss the following things about your story with your teacher:

Who are the characters?
Where does the story take place?
What problem or conflict do the characters face?
How do they solve the problem?

Example: Characters - The Three Pigs
Setting - forest, out on their own
Problem - making houses, safe from wolf
Solution - a brick house, hot water

Use the next few days to complete your story.

TEACHER'S NOTE: This story can be ywo paragraphs or a book. You determine what your child is ready to produce in this type of writing.

OPTIONS: a)   Write two paragraphs including all the above components.
b)   Write two paragraphs, with one on each page and an illustration on each one.
c)   Write three - six paragraphs with few or no illustrations.
d)   Write three - six paragraphs. Use the Book Making Unit and create a book of the story complete with illustrations.

Teacher Helps:

2.   **b.**   the dog

       c.   Possible Answer: **simple:** not complex, having few parts

             Possible Answers: **easy:** not hard to do; free from pain

             Possible Answer: Herkimer's advice is not complex; it is <u>simply</u> to love the dog. But loving a dog can be a hard, painful thing to do if you are afraid of dogs.

TEACHER'S NOTE: This activity may take two days.

1.   There are many different ways to take your work and bind it, or put it in a more permanent cover. We have already introduced a few ways to organize the information you have gathered and make it look nice. Look in a reference book or at the library for the topic of bookbinding. Can you find anything out about the history of bookbinding? Also look for different examples of what is meant by Japanese bookbinding.

2.   You will now be given some steps for binding a book in a style similar to Japanese bookbinding. This activity will take at least several days, possibly one-two weeks. You may take the information gathered in the journal unit on your family and make that into a book. You may also want to create a bound book using the report you did on your state or a story you created. There is no limit to the kinds of books you can make. Have fun creating your book, and then you will be an author and a bookmaker.

TEACHER'S NOTE: Because of the use of contact cement, sewing needles and scissors, we feel that this must be a teacher-supervised activity.

Step 1:   Materials you will need:
a)   medium weight paper (maybe 20 lb in any color that will make your book look nice)
b)   stiff cardboard
c)   scissors
d)   white glue or contact cement
e)   stapler or needle (large needle with sharp point)
f)   heavy thread (such as quilting, rug, or binding thread)
g)   cloth, contact paper, or wallpaper
h)   cloth tape or adhesive tape
i)   ruler

Step 2: After you finish writing and illustrating your work add a table of contents (if you want) and a title page to the front of your work. If any bibliography is needed, add that to the end. Add a blank sheet of paper to the front and back of your work. You are now ready to staple or sew your pages together. Staple or sew the pages approximately 1/4 inch from the edge. If you are going to sew the pages, use the ruler to mark six points on a guide sheet of paper, evenly distributed. (See diagram below) With your teacher's help use the guide sheet to punch a hole through your paper using your needle.

Make a single strand (double strand if the pages seem thick) of about 24 inches. Weave the thread in and out as diagramed below. Tie a knot in the end when completed.

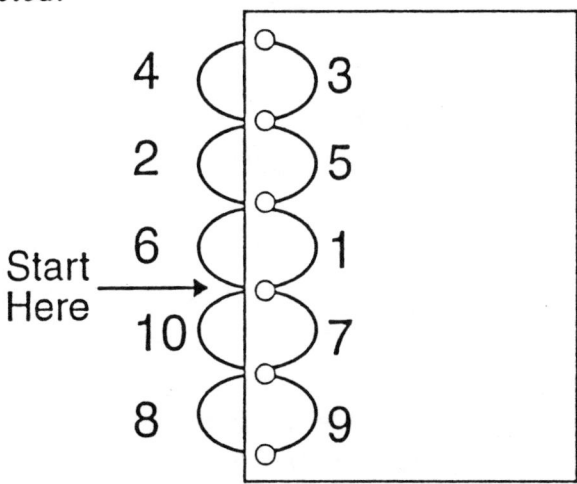

Step 3: Cut two pieces of cardboard at least 3/4 inch larger than your pages on three sides (see diagram below).

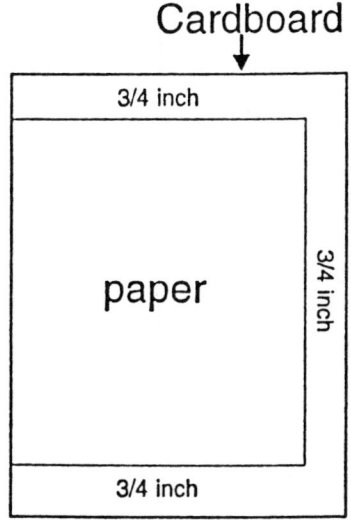

Cut a cardboard strip 1/2 inch wide and the same length as the other cardboard pieces. Tape the two cardboard sides to the end strip. Here's a diagram:

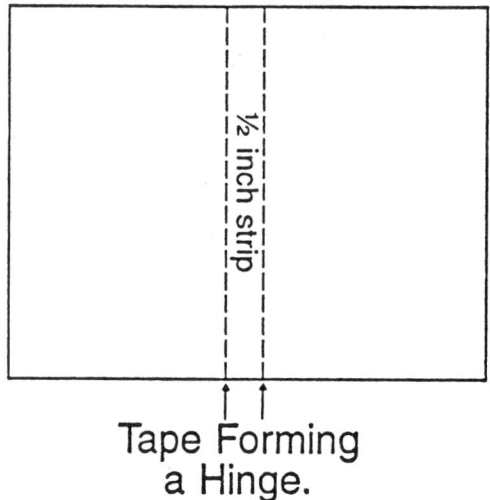

Tape Forming
a Hinge.

Step 4: Choose the type of material you want to use for a cover: cloth, contact paper or wallpaper. After choosing your cover material, cut a piece approximately 1 inch larger than your cardboard covers.

Step 5: Place the cover material face down. Place glue or contact cement on the cardboard cover or peel the backing off the contact paper. You may need your teacher to help with contact paper, because it may roll up when the backing is removed. Make sure and place your cardboard cover in the center of the material. Place your cardboard cover on top of the cover material and press down.

Cover material of your choice.

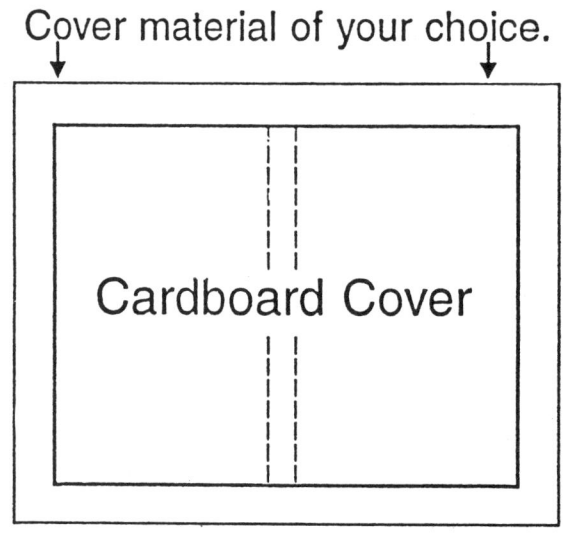

Step 6: Using a ruler, draw a diagonal line from the diagram below and trim along that line. This will make the folds smooth and look nicer.

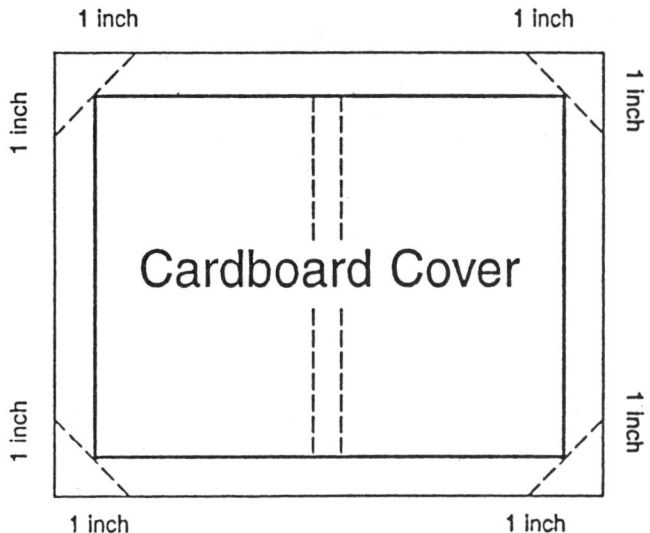

Place glue or contact cement lightly on the edges of your cardboard covers and fold over one at a time. Press gently and wipe off any excess glue.

Step 7: Place the book pages over the cardboard covers, lining them up in the center. Glue the back page down to the cover and press gently to smooth the page. Glue the front page down to the cover and press gently to smooth the pages. Wipe off any excess glue. If you have chosen to tape the cardboard covers together 1/2 inch apart, you may want to place your book under a stack of heavy books to press it down and make it flatter.

Step 8: If you would like, a card with the title of your book or a picture can be glued to the front of your book.

Now you can share this book with family and friends! You can follow these steps with any material you'd like to make into a book.

"Student Editing Models"

1

"What a beautiful place!" said Violet.
"Henry!" cried Jessie. "Let's live here!"
"Live here?" asked Henry.
"Yes! Why not?" said Jessie. "This boxcar is a fine little house. It is dry and warm in the rain."

2

That same night Dr. Moore sat reading the paper. All at once he saw the word LOST and began to read.

"LOST. Four children, two boys and two girls. Somewhere around Greenfield or Silver City. Five thousand dollars to anyone who can find them.

James Henry Alden."

3

The children's grandfather wanted them to like his house. He wanted them to live with him all the time. So he had made over some of the rooms just for them.

The children went with him in his car to see the house. When the car stopped in front of it, Henry cried in surprise, "Do you live *here*, in this beautiful house?"

9

The Wright boys were friendly. It didn't take them long to get acquainted with the boys on Adams Street in Cedar Rapids, Iowa.

They were getting acquainted with the city too. Today they had gone to see the rapids in the Cedar River. They were standing on the bank now looking down at the whirling water.

10

It was Wilbur's act in the Wright and Johnston Circus that started the stilt craze in Richmond. By the time a week had passed, several boys had made stilts and were learning to use them.

Orville and Gansey were working on theirs. Wilbur was helping them. He showed them how to make foot rests and where to fasten them to the poles.

11

Then came the great moment. They carried the glider to the top of the dune. Wilbur climbed on the lower wing and lay face-down. He grasped the bar that would move the wing tips. Orville began to loosen the ropes.

In spite of its load, the machine rose off the sand and up into the air, about eight feet. The brothers forgot their hours of hard work. The glider had lifted! Their ideas had been right, even if it did come down after a few seconds.

Matt stood at the edge of the clearing for some time after his father had gone out of sight among the trees. There was just a chance that his father might turn back, that perhaps he had forgotten something or had some last word of advice. This was one time Matt reckoned he wouldn't mind the advice, no matter how many times he had heard it before. But finally he had to admit that this was not going to happen. His father had really gone. He was alone, with miles of wilderness stretching on every side.

from <u>The Sign of the Beaver</u> by Elizabeth George Speare. Copy right (c) 1983 by Elizabeth George Speare. Reprinted by permission of Houghton Mifflin Co. All rights reserved.

22

He turned and looked back at the log house. It was a fair house, he thought; his mother would have no cause to be ashamed of it. He had helped to build every inch of it. He had helped to cut down the spruce trees and haul the logs and square and notch them. He had stood at one end of every log and raised it, one on top of the other, fitting the notched ends together as snugly as though they had grown that way. **He had climbed the roof to fasten down the cedar splint with long poles, and dragged up pine boughs to cover them. Behind the cabin were the mounds of corn he had helped to plant, the green blades already shooting up, and the pumpkin vines just showing between the stumps of trees.**

23

He was sitting on the flat stone that served as a doorstep, waiting for his supper to cook. The late sun slanted in long yellow bars across the clearing. The forest beyond was already in shadow. **Matt was feeling well pleased with his day. That morning he had shot a rabbit. He had skinned it carefully, stretching the fur against the cabin wall to dry.**

29

Before Uncle Alfred could answer, there arose the most tremendous ruckus: a big, booming roar. HAR-ROOMF! Easily, the most thrilling and frightening noise Anabelle had ever heard. And the loudest. HAR-ROOMF! HAR-ROOMF! HAR-R-R-ROO-MM-FF!

It sounded like ... like ... the young hedgehog did not know *what* it sounded like. She had never heard anything *like* it before in her short life.

"What was that?" Anabelle asked, turning wide eyes to the far bank of the canal. The big, booming noise was coming from across the water.

30

"It means," replied the elder hedgehog, "that you simply put yourself in the dog's place, and think how you would like someone to behave towards you."

"But I don't know the first thing about being a dog," young Anabelle pointed out. "I don't know the first thing about anything, really."

31

"It's very simple," Herkimer told her. "To turn an enemy into a friend, all you have to do is love him."

"Love him? Are you sure? That doesn't sound easy at all. That sounds terribly difficult to me."

"Oh, it is difficult," Herkimer agreed. "Probably one of the most difficult things in the world. But I said it was simple, not easy."

SKILLS INDEX

Composition

Capitalization - 2, 9, 29
Commas - 9, 19, 27
Dialogue - 1
Envelopes - 8, 27
Exclamation points - 1, 30
Friendly letters - 8, 27
Illustrating Poetry - 17, 18, 19
Illustrating Stories - 31
Italics - 3, 29
Journal Writing - 24, 25, 26, 28

Newspaper Writing - 5, 6, 7
Note-taking - 8
Paragraphs - 5, 6, 7
Periods - 1, 29
Poetry Writing - 15
Quotation Marks - 1, 30
Question Marks - 1
Sentence Structure - 9, 10, 11, 21, 22, 23
Similes - 18
Story Writing - 9, 11, 30

Comprehension

Autobiography/Biography - 9
Context - 31
Fact/Opinion - 6
Memorizing Poetry - 17
8, 12, 14

Poetry/Prose - 18
Rhyme in Poetry - 15, 16, 18
Rhythm in Poetry - 15, 16
Vocabulary Development - 4, 5

Grammar

Abbreviations - 2, 3
Adjectives - 1, 2, 16, 18, 19, 21, 22, 23, 25
Adverbs - 23
Alphabetizing - 14
Antoayms - 1
Articles - 30
Common nouns - 2
Comparisons - 29
Conjunctions - 22
First Person - 9
Helping Verbs - 10, 23
Helping Nouns - 1, 2, 10, 22
Past Tense - 11

Phrases - 9, 15
Possessive nouns - 3
Possessive pronouns - 3
Prepositions - 9, 10
Present tense - 11
Pronouns - 3
Proper nouns - 2
Syllables - 18, 29
Synonyms - 18
Suffix - 11, 21
Third person - 9
Verbs - 10, 11, 16, 18, 22, 25

Study Skills

BIBLIOGRAPHY

Lawhead, Stephen, <u>The Tale of Anabelle Hedgehog</u>, 1705 Hubbard Avenue, Batavia, Illinois, 60510: Lion Publishing Corporation, 1990.

Speare, Elizabeth George, <u>The Sign of the Beaver</u>, 215 Park Avenue South, New York, New York, 10003: Houghton Mifflin Company, 1983.

Stevenson, Augusta, <u>Wilbur and Orville Wright</u>, 866 Third Avenue, New York, New York, 10022: Macmillan Publishing Company, 1984.

Stevenson, Augusta, <u>Benjamin Franklin</u>, 866 Third Avenue, New York, New York, 10022: Macmillan Publishing Company.

Warner, Gertrude Chandler, <u>The Boxcar Children</u>, 6340 Oakton Street, Morton Grove, Illinois, 60053: Albert Whitman and Company.